Ethnogenesis

Foundations of Thought and Action

Eduardo Seda Bonilla, Ph.D.

Note for Librarians: a cataloguing record for this book that includes Dewey Decimal Classification and US Library of Congress numbers is available from the Library and Archives of Canada. The complete cataloguing record can be obtained from their online database at:
www.collectionscanada.ca/amicus/index-e.html
ISBN 1-4120-5126-6

TRAFFORD

Offices in Canada, USA, Ireland, UK and Spain
This book was published *on-demand* in cooperation with Trafford Publishing. On-demand publishing is a unique process and service of making a book available for retail sale to the public taking advantage of on-demand manufacturing and Internet marketing. On-demand publishing includes promotions, retail sales, manufacturing, order fulfilment, accounting and collecting royalties on behalf of the author.
Book sales for North America and international:
Trafford Publishing, 6E–2333 Government St.,
Victoria, BC v8t 4p4 CANADA
phone 250 383 6864 (toll-free 1 888 232 4444)
fax 250 383 6804; email to orders@trafford.com
Book sales in Europe:
Trafford Publishing (uk) Ltd., Enterprise House, Wistaston Road Business Centre, Wistaston Road, Crewe, Cheshire cw2 7rp UNITED KINGDOM
phone 01270 251 396 (local rate 0845 230 9601)
facsimile 01270 254 983; orders.uk@trafford.com
Order online at:
www.trafford.com/robots/05-0021.html

10 9 8 7 6 5 4 3

Since it is in the mind of people where wars are born,
it is in the mind of people where peace must be found.

United Nations Declaration on Culture for Peace

ACKNOWLEDGEMENT

My sincerest and deepest thanks to Olga Jeffery whose generous dedication made possible the publication of this book.

Cover photo by Leopold van Quarles.

TABLE OF CONTENTS

"Together let us explore the stars, conquer the deserts, eradicate disease, tap the oceans depths, and the glow from the fire can truly light the world."

John F. Kennedy

Jan. 20 1961

The means of transportation and communication in the modern world, have advanced to a point where distances are shortened and the planet is reduced to a world village. The fancy of Jules Verne to travel, "Around the World in Eighty Days," is no longer a big challenge, considering that spy satellites travel around the planet several times a day. At the same moment a volcano erupts on Mount Etna, a fire burns the woodlands of California, a flood afflicts the poor people of Central America, an earthquake destroys Mexico City, the Egyptians celebrate a new millennium, an airplane crashes in Long Island, a beatification takes place in the Vatican, or civilians are killed in the streets of Baghdad it is witnessed by most people of the world "live and in full color," The Gulf War was waged in front of the television cameras. The atrocities of war can be seen first hand. The depth of the sea, the height of the Himalayas, the descent of the astronauts on the surface of the moon, far away planets, the Amazon jungle, are now observable by everyone.

Television brings to our living rooms, geniuses of intellect and art, classical concerts with major orchestras, potentates of international politics, athletic events, as passionate as the Olympics, excellent movies. Reality is transformed by the human intellect with computer technology, the internet, robots, commercial and weather satellites, clones to make duplicates of bodies or body parts to replace damage organs. Women can purchase on-line, ova to fertilize with sperm, science progresses in the branch of genetic engineering, making it now possible, and placing near at hand, the dream of Ponce de Leon or Faust for eternal youth.

Airports are filled with passengers, traveling in all directions, in a sort of dreamlike escape from reality. There are space shuttles capable of interplanetary travel. However, where is humanization? Emotional intelligence is not developing at the speed of science technology. The means toward humanization have not evolved in comparable manner with the means of exploiting and controlling nature. We live in a world of midgets of emotion and giants of intellect. Emotional illiteracy runs side by side with the horses of the Apocalypse, leading to the worst kind of human impoverishment. Caliban, the polymorph perverse of the unconscious, disseminates darkness, a vomit of fire manifested in brutal incidents of criminality. We harvest the storms of criminality with a toll of casualties equivalent to a civil war.

All property is in danger of plunder. The kingdom of terror contaminates the environment with distrust and insensitivity. An army of mercenaries force the people to live behind iron bars. A terrifying reality emerges. There are high rates of alcoholism, with figures of murders that compare to the figures from war. Robbers assault passersbys on the streets in full light, and those who resists the assault, are killed without any contemplation. Pornography competes for profits with the sale of arms and narcotics. Emotional problems are multiplied in depression, alcoholism, drug addiction, and crime. Values are substituted by ideologies.

The development of thinking at its optimum potentialities is necessary to halt the prospect of a super technology alien to human values. A dehumanized robot made his appearance more than fifty years ago in Nazi Germany, causing desolation, pain, death, — the infamous genocide of the Jewish people. It is insanity not to face the conditions of the learning environment, (didactogenesis) which are debased by existing trends toward emotional illiteracy.

It is imperative, for the survival of humanity, to put an end to genocidal wars, stopping the rapacity in international relations and the destruction of woodlands, especially the Amazonian forest, which are the lungs of the planet. There must be a halt to the contamination of the environment and the atmosphere, to injustice, hatred, and the irrationality present in a lumpenized world. Poverty extends over the face of the planet, yet superpowers have the capability of extermination of humanity with multimillionaire military budgets.

There is informative television. However, there is also another type of television in Puerto Rico that brings mostly trash into our homes. Witchcraft apprentices, armed with the S-R technology, exhibit half dressed celebrities, to promote consumerism. These sexy celebrities show their nakedness, as means toward success, becoming role models for our youth.

In a speech in the tomb of its father, Don Luis Muñoz Marin, who mandated the history of Puerto Rico for many years, expressed his disappointment with material prosperity, if it is lacking in values. "The material prosperity in itself cannot be the ideal of a people. The material prosperity is a means — is the pedestal of the statue, but is not the statue. The statue is the image held in the hearts of the people —in the virtues of liberty and justice." In the abolition of emotional illiteracy lies the solution. That is the subject of this writing.

CHAPTER 1

Epistemic Foundations of Cognition

*The world we want to build is one where we see creative
spirit, where life is filled with adventure of fundamental hope
and the impulse to construct, and not in the desire to hold
what one possesses or remove another's possessions.
It is a world where liberty flows, and love sheds the impulse
of domination, and cruelty, and envy, and substitutes them for
happiness.*

Bertrand Russell

Do you remember the last time a mote fell in one of your eyes? The discomfort was intolerable because no object of the material world can enter, as such, in the sensory organs of sight, touch, hearing, smelling, etc. Objects are out there while you, the observer, are here. From objects, we have the image, selected on the basis of the epistemic foundation.

The epistemic foundations are the underlying assumptions, the premise upon which cognition stands.. In between the sense organs and the external world there are epistemic lenses, that select out that which fits the underlying assumptions, leaving out that which does not fit those assumptions. Selective perception is known as,' gestalt.' Perception is selective, and action conforms to perception.

An anecdote of two drunks in the Bowery, illustrates the function of selective perception. One of the drunks looks at a bottle of cheap wine and sees, "a bottle half full." The other dissents. He sees a half empty bottle.

In my student days, I heard many heated debates between those who argued that what causes social change is the borrowing from one culture to another, and those who conceived social change as a product of evolution. There were also the Whiteans, arguing that technology is the motor of social change, while Marxists conceived culture as an ideological superstructure to fit the mode of production. There were orthodox freudians, neofreudians, adlerians, jungians, rogerians, proposing different brands of psycho analysis, and in some cases claiming an exclusive constituency. These different angles of observation would enrich knowledge, if not assumed as dogma.

George Kelly, in his book, *Psychology of Personal Constructs*, said, "Every perception has its point of departure in a previous belief." The previous belief is, of course, the epistemic foundation or paradigm. "A mind without such previous beliefs or epistemic foundations is an empty mind," says Talcott Parsons, using instead the term 'theory'. "If one does not know what one is searching for, one would not recognize nor give a correct reading to what one finds," says Claude Bernard. A folk expression confirms "He /she who does not know is the same as he who does not see."

Since the time when Thomas Khun published, *The Rise of Scientific Revolutions*, (Chicago, U. of Chicago Press, 1970) the epistemic foundation that stand between perception and reality has been known as paradigms. In his book, there are epoch making paradigms such as the universe of Tolomeo, or that of Copernicus, or that of Newton, or the Einsteinian. Galileo's ideas collided with those that served as a looking glass to the Inquisition. The Inquisition tribunals accused him of heresy. He could not see so simple a truth as the sun moving around the earth. Feudalism, Renaissance, modern world, and today's information world, are universes with a particular psycho-syllogistic way of conceiving reality and thus of collective action. There are historical periods that have left an imprint on the history of ideas, such as the Greeks of the epoch of Pericles, and the Italian Renaissance. In the history of art there was the Baroque period, characterized by a full expression of emotions, movement, and color, alternating with the Classical period, characterized by delicacy and refinement in expression.

Ethnology is a sort of virtual museum of culture which encompass the collective epistemic system that informs the creation of reality of peoples. The world of the Tainos, who inhabited Puerto Rico before the arrival of the Europeans, was governed by deities of the land, the sun, the moon, the rain, the wind, the rivers, the mountains, the "sky", etc. They were subjects of that kingdom and had to pay the tribute of worship to those deities and propitiate them with rites, offerings, and sacrifices. This polytheism, at least as poetry, might be well taken by today's conservationists, who are concerned with the protection of our natural environment.

What distinguishes one epoch from another are the patterns of cognition that inform actions made on the basis of "epistemic foundations." When epistemes are valid formulae, they operate as lenses for an ever increasing fund of knowledge in the history of ideas. The lowest possible validity of an epistemic configuration is naive realism — the confusion of the image (in here) with the thing in itself (out there). Higher up on the scale of validity there is critical thinking, leading to the most sophisticated theories of science and artistic creations.

Some years ago I was driving down a steep hill of Cerro Maravilla and suddenly the car engine stopped in the middle of the road. Lifting the hood to look at the motor it was as if I were looking at the pyramids of Egypt. I did not see what the mechanic who came to repair it saw immediately.

In the absence of a paradigm, some improvise. In unawareness of open paradigmatic roads, improvising often results in inventing tepid water or discovering the Mediterranean. Guey Sorman, in *The True Thinkers of Our Time,* says that, "in ignorance one may see chaos where one who knows sees integrated parts." Once the logogenic light enters the darkness, mystery disappear. "Behind the apparent quantum (chaos) he adds, "there is a cause determining what we do not know. To accept that the world is incomprehensible is to brag about our lack of understanding."

Charles Peirce classified the configurations of selective perception along a continuum, from the icon, the sign, and the highest attainable level where critical thinking is possible, the symbol.

Icons:
An icon is a facsimile, an effigy, a photograph or any

other graphic representation. Icons are best known as sacred images in churches. Ideographic discourse is a literal account, as in history, ethnography, and anecdotal journalism. To be a completely accurate and exact ideographic representation, it would need to occupy the same space at the same time as that which it represents. Apart from being impossible, this would have no practical value. Ideographic accounts contrast with the nomothetic, the latter being a high level critical abstraction. Nomos, in this case, means logos or epistemic foundations. Logos signify knowledge, mind, intelligence, and comprehension.(Webster, Unabridged, 1977, pg. 1225)

Today, there are "painters" who smear paint on paper or on canvas, as a child or a crazy person does, in a sort of acting out at the ideograph plane. These paintings can be made by an elephant, or a monkey. Rorschach cards produce responses comparable to those elicited by such paintings. The contents of Rorschach cards are ink blots. The response is a function of repressed unconscious sources.

Signs:

Signs can be arranged in two contrasting categories. There are those that are integrated in a theoretical system functioning as indicators, such as the height of a column of mercury indicating temperature in a thermometer. There is an infinite repertoire of indicators in the field of medicine, mechanics, electronics, cybernetics, high technology, and space engineering.

In Pavlov's experiments, a bell was rung and then food was presented to a dog. At some point, after a number of trials called reinforcements in behavioral theory, the dog responded to the bell as if it were food.

Applied to human behavior, S-R (stimulus response) is used to implant automaticities. Those who control the didactogenic sources of cognition in a society have, in S-R automaticities, an effective weapon. A pleasurable stimulation, placed in contiguity to a neutral stimulation, pervades and permeates the contiguous neutral stimulus with its pleasurable sensations. H. Mower, in his book, *Behavior and the Symbolic Process*, (New York, Wiley, 1965) traces the S-R method to 15th century Lazarillo de Tormes, who had to share the scarce mouthfuls his master gave him with hungry cats. In front of his master there was nothing that he could do to scare away the hungry begging cats. However, in the absence of his master, Lazarillo clapped his hands and followed the clapping with a thrashing of the cats. Once the S-R connection between hand clapping and punishment was established all he had to do to disperse the hungry cats was to produce a dissimulated hand clap.. In this way he could enjoy his miserable fare.

Machiavelli systematized this old notion into a theory of government. Positive reinforcements consisting of enticement with bribery produces good will on the governed and thus stability to the government of the Prince. For those who do not accept bribery there are negative reinforcements, stretching out from doors closed to employment, refused promotion, to the trademark of hard hand regimes, which is terror like that of Pinochet in Chile, Fascist Germany, Spain, Trujllo, The Chacal of the Caribbean, The Inquisition, McCarthyism etc.

In everyday life there are experts in imprinting S-R

automaticities as a amusement. Children in my home village had a good command of the S-R formula. These little rascals used it as a teasing game called, "a nickel," like in the nickelodeon, (echarle un vellon). When the time of the Patron Saint Festival was near, a comment was dropped casually to be overheard by a person who was a bit retarded. The remark was, "the Patron Saint Festival has been suspended." A tirade of profanities was the response. There was a woman, somewhat mentally deranged, who the children, on their way home from school, would often meet on the street. The trigger was the word, "Phew." The automatic response on the part of the woman consisted in lifting her skirt.. This automatic response never failed. An Italian film, "8 1/2," reminded me of this incident.

Programmers of collective didactogenesis use S-R automaticity as social engineering technology for the purpose of manipulating the learning environment. Vance Packard in his book, *The Hidden Persuaders,* (New York; McKay 1957) has a critical statement against this manipulative social technology to increase consumerism.

Social scientists, of the highest technical caliber, have learned from experiments with rats, in the laboratories of behaviorist psychology, that a pleasure stimulus, placed in contiguity to a neutral stimulus, (for example, a bell and the food) pervades and permeates the neutral stimulus. After a number of trials the response provoked by food in Pavlov's experiments is transferred to the sound of the bell preceding the food presentation

A beautiful women, in scanty clothing, is presented next to a market product, thus eliciting an appetite that is transferred to the product by associative contagion. The erotic appeal provokes an appetite that is transferred to many products, such as alcoholic beverages, cars, clothes etc. These acquire, by associative contagion, the attraction that in fact belongs to the beautiful sex symbols or sex workers who make a living doing commerce with their bodies.

A lot more space is given to the attractive young lady in the bathtub than to the product itself in commercials for soap. Candidates are sold the same way soap is sold on television advertisements. Things that have nothing to do with one another are "read" as if they were intrinsically related.

Causality by association, such as guilt by association, was used in the MaCarthy era, bringing about a witch hunt in which people like Robert Oppenheimer, who had been the director of the Los Alamos project in which the atom bomb was produced, as well as many actors, were stigmatized and marginalized. What Freud called, unconscious, is the fountainhead of irrational action, implanted as S-R automaticities in moments of extreme pain, loss, despair, etc. When the associative S-R automaticity begins to substitute conceptual critical thinking in a society, the imbecility, that Ortega y Gasset called 'mass society," begins. We have used the term, 'lumpenization' in reference to a sector of the modern world which has lost the ability to think with critical concepts, with a prevalence of S-R simplicity. In such a society, critical concepts are deemed "difficult" and uppity.

Ken Wilber, in his book, *The Quest for New Paradigm*, (Boston, Shambala,1990) has written that, "In this model (behaviorist), the person has no choice. Choice is possible where there is awareness of alternatives. The person exposed to S-R push button reaction has no free will, no proaction, no choice. This model works very well with animal levels of human beings. Animals are indeed pre-symbolic, pre-intentional, prehistoric, and pre-volitional. Classical behaviorism works rather poorly with human beings because human beings possess, between the sensory stimuli and the sensory response, a mental structure,(epistemes) and that structure obeys laws whose actions are not perceptual but intelligent. Trying to handle these mental phenomenological data (discourse, dialogue, communication, introspection, hermeneutics, phenomenology) with empirical methods,. for instance, by calling them 'verbal behavior', is about as effective as trying to discover the meaning of 'War and Peace' by analyzing the objective paper and ink on which it is expressed."

Symbols

The ascent into the nature of reality, through symbolic representation, is an event of such transcendental importance as for A. R..Luria, in the book, *Language and Thought*, to state that the change from the sensorial (S-R) modality, as a mode of insertion into the world of reality, to the symbolic mode, constitutes" a leap that alters, to such an extent the psychic activity, that the classics of the materialistic philosophy considered this event as important as the leap from inanimate existence to life." The epistemic foundation from which symbolic configurations of thought are derived, can be submitted to critical analysis of their validity as well as their reliability

There are differences in the configuration of perception which stem from the angle of vision. German sociology uses the term, "gestalt" in reference to the perceptual configuration produced by the selective perception caused by epistemic premises. In his book, *Study of Man,* Ralph Linton illustrates the variations in perception according to the epistemic lenses used to ascertain an object. "A piece of rock," says Linton, "is a hammer for the farmer needing to repair a fallen fence. The geologist, with epistemic eyeglasses from science, sees the rock as a relic of pre- history. A new David sees the rock as a weapon of attack. A piece of wood, in the eyes of an artisan, is raw material for carving. For a castaway on high sea, the piece of wood would be seen as a life saver. For a camping person in a park, the piece of wood would be seen as firewood.

What reality is in one culture is not necessarily the reality of another culture. J.S. Bruner, describes in his book, *A Study of Thinking,* (New York, Wiley,) profound differences in perception and the action emanating from the epistemic foundations of different cultures. These differences are the subject matter of ethnology. Ethnology is a virtual museum of cultures.

The underlying epistemic foundation in reference, let us say to color perception, varies from one culture to another. The Bassa of Nigeria, according to Jerome Bruner, have two categories of color. The Shona of Liberia have four colors. There is no doubt that if in the epistemic foundation of these cultures, other colors were discriminated, the perception of the people would include those other colors. M. D. Vernon tells us that the inhabitants of Fiji do not distinguish green from blue, and the Kaffirs have twenty-six descriptive terms of color to distinguish their cattle. The Eskimos have three different names for snow. In Puerto Rico, those who take care of fighting cocks distinguish colors in the feathers of the roosters that do not exist in the rest of the community. Camaguey, bulico, etc. are unknown colors among the non initiated.

The epistemic foundation that determines the perception of consonants among the Chinese does not differentiate /L/ from /R/ which provides ground for the quip "alo flito" for arroz frito (fried rice). Arabs do not learn to distinguish /p/ from /b/ ground for the quip of the Arab salesman who asks the good lady for 'un beso' for the merchandise sold. In the absence of the differentiation between/p/ and /b/ 'peso', a dollar, becomes 'beso' a kiss.

Beyond the territory of reality there are doors to enter unreality, such as chimeras, rhetorical fancy, fiction, ideology, etc. There is a range of epistemic foundations determining emotions, starting at the heights of enthusiasm, and going down in a gradual trend to the doldrums of apathy, passing in a middle range of boredom, combativeness, propitiation etc. Far beyond the doors to enter the fanciful territory of fiction there are doors to enter the labyrinth of hallucinations and perceptual distortions, described in Chapter IX as Acting Out.

The blessing of freedom in the awareness of option is not always fully enjoyed and remains as a possibility. There are "complexes", schotoma, amnesia, and other irrational automatisms. Schotoma is a point in the eye that lacks vision. This term was formulated by anthropologist psychoanalyst, Gregory Bateson. Harry Stack Sullivan used the term "Selective inattention" for the exclusion and inclusion in perception. A person may refuse to see, as stated in the aphorism,' that the worst blind man is the one who refuses to see'.

The idea that entrance into the mystery of reality is informed by epistemic foundations lost credibility in an epoch when there was a total reaction against grandiose formulations that were not supported by empirical confirmation, such as evolutionism, diffusionism etc. Franz Boas, of Columbia University in New York, proclaimed hard data as the only valid currency in the professional world of anthropology. The "hardness," I suppose, is in the eyes of the beholder with shared epistemic foundations.

American psychology brought forth the hard data of S-R behaviorism. Epistemic foundations would enter by the back door since, as said above, there is no cognition which is not informed by an epistemic foundation. Rene Thom labeled radical empiricism, "a junk yard." Alien to theory, such as the well known' palos a ciegas', (hit and miss praxis) discovers tepid water or the Mediterranean, ignoring how far back that discovery was made. Science rejects dogmatism as well as empty rhethoricism or the crude empiricism that refuses to acknowledge the epistemic foundations from where data proceeds. Untested formulations or hypothesis must be exposed to the test of falsification, as Karl Popper would say, so as to be admitted in the category of theory. Elegance is not a criterion. The most beautiful theory, if it does not resist an empirical test, is ruled out.

A culture to be discussed, in next chapter, as the totality of configurations of perceptions that inform the collective awareness, of "we the people."

CHAPTER II

Cultural Construction of Reality

Culture is the cup where people drink the water of life
quoted by Ruth Benedict

The maternal womb gives breath and life to the body. Culture is a second womb in the formation and development of human beings. Language communication, the web of social relations, and survival skills, are shared with our fellow human beings, since they are acquired in enculturation

Deprived of enculturation, a child may have the human form but will lack the essential condition of being human. A child deprived of enculturation, as said of feral children in India, lacks the essential human condition embodied in language communication, the skills to partake in the web of social relations and survival skill.(Joseph Amrito Lai and Robert Zingg, *Wolf Children and Feral Man, Hamden*, Conn.,Archor Books, 1996.) Pitirim Sorokin, to these effects, wrote: "If any one of us were isolated at birth from human contacts, how much of our culture could one discover by oneself? The simplest rules of addition and subtraction, the elementary notion of physics and biology the use of simple tools, like the level, the wheel, the bow and arrow, or the production and use of fire, easily learned by a boy of seven, would exceed the ability of one hundred percent of us, even if we lived one hundred years and had the brain of Sir Isaac Newton."

Outside of culture, as implied by Aristotle's aphorism, only animals and gods may survive. Professor Alfred Kroeber of Columbia University, used to say that a kitten raised among dogs will never learn to bark, to lift his leg on a light post, or to wag his tail as a token of friendship. Today's cat is the same cat as Cleopatra's, centuries and centuries past. Animals behavior pertains to the realm of genetics, plus sundry automatisms implanted by the S-R method. Intentionality, responsibility, creative action, freedom, awareness of choice, causality, are attributes that pertain only to human beings. Patterns of collaboration with one another in affinity and solidarity are acquired in enculturation. What one generation borrows from the data bank of culture is, in most cases, returned with "interest." Don Jose Ortega y Gasset states the notion of ethnogenesis in these words, "Man does not have nature. He has history." History is the ever flowing river of ethnogenesis.

We are the heirs of Prometheus who stole the fire of from the gods and gave it to human beings. Enlightenment, in the fire of cognition, liberated man, to a great extent, from genetically inherited automatisms, characteristics of animals. In turn, it brought upon his/her shoulders awareness of being the cause of intended effect with responsibility for creations. Therefore, every minute of his/her life became a journey from preexistence to an existence to be attained as option in the vehicle of projects. The responsibility for the creation in the vehicle of projects made him/her, as Sartre has said, a slave of freedom. Freedom in option became unavoidable. He /she who avoids taking an option, has opted in that way"says Sartre. Every minute of human life is option Options, on that river of decisional processes, are as present as the air we breathe.

Ethnogenesis became the foundation of humanization. The totality of options, in an ever flowing ethnogenic river of decisional projects, constitutes biography for individuals and history for people. Epistemic configurations began its upward advance providing new vision of what is ahead -a new scaffold for further advance in knowledge and mastery of reality. Planning is the substance of human life. The planned construction of reality began with the invention of language. Language is the tool to represent in the mind what is possible in the world of reality. Language is the map, as Korsibski called it, 'the image in the mind' that always can be improved along a path that never ends. Language is the greatest achievement in human history.

Fire, hunting devices, stone tools, and then the domestication of plants and animals brought forth the choice for a sedentary life in a civil society Primitive villages became towns, then cities, empires, states, nations, with a technology that has progressed to the conquest of the atom, cybernetics, clonation. The super power, generated by the informatic era, in the hands of witchcraft apprentices, endangers survival of the planet. The hope rests in the option of emotional education.

One must return what one borrows from the ethnogenic fountain source with interest. "We stand on the shoulders of giants who preceded us" said Newton. (Robert K. Merton,

On the Shoulders of Giants, Glencoe Free Press.) On the shoulders of giants that preceded us, we must move on in history in an eternal ascent.

"A creature of its own creation," as Marx said, "makes man the eternal traveler, improving what he /she has received as seed for further tillage."

To plan is to assume an option among many.. Options, as said above, are inevitable. Every day reality is constructed according to representation based on the epistemic foundations of values or ideologies of culture. The epistemic foundation of values is the genesis of self actualization. The epistemic foundation of ideologies leads to destruction and invalidation of human potentialities.. Planning for the attainment of optimal human potentialities must consider that if the seed we plant is ideology, the harvest is confusion, chaos, and dehumanization. Humanistic planning for self actualization must be based on a foundation of values. The authority of governments could be well used to exalt existence if there were a better understanding of culture and its foundations. Values on the one hand and ideologies on the other.. Ideologies, are the epistemic foundations of evil. The eternal advance, inherent to culture, shrinks back in the recesses of obscurantism, where ideology takes control of collective decisional processes.

When planning of decisional processes is conduced, on the basis of values as epistemic foundations, it provides the conditions for self actualization at the personal and collective level. Values are the source of creative intelligence, enthusiasm, generosity, altruism, and all the treasures and richness of a culture. This treasure is the cumulative creation of all generations of the past. For the governing bodies, whose legislation and interpretation of the laws and public administration create decisional processes resulting in the construction of reality, a didactogenic awareness is essential Ennobling human existence is today a possibility. Visionaries, like our Hostos, conceived the road to happiness as creative action with a foundation in values.

At this moment, it is not utopian to expect the planning of enculturation aimed towards the elevation of the human condition. A government can not afford to ignore the effect produced by its planning, positive, negligent, or oppressive.

Robert Redfield defined culture as "shared understanding." Shared epistemic foundations of a culture contain the cumulative knowledge obtained along the path of history. Life flows in the river of planned agenda. The analogy of life as a river goes back to ancient times, to Heraclito and to poets like Jorge Manrique. Poets, like Antonio Machado, prefer the analogy of life as a road, "Yo voy soñando caminos de la tarde.." Our poet, Juan Antonio Corretjer, wrote a poem, "En la Vida Todo es Ir" (life is always going.)

Edward B. Tyler, founder of cultural anthropology, defined culture as that complex whole that includes, "customs, art, religion, language and those skills and capabilities acquired by human beings as a member of society." These capabilities emanate from epistemic foundations that inform the way of seeing and acting. The cup of life, as said before, of primitive societies, assesses their reality in terms of five epistemic domains. These are decency, morality, aesthetics, religion, and adhoc improvisation. Modern societies add to these political culture and science. Science is the hottest of all modern paradigms of culture. Specific values, such as honesty, generosity, integrity, consideration to fellow humans, sincerity, righteousness, modesty, etc. belong to morality and decency. The religious paradigm includes values such as devotion, faith, abnegation, mercy, resignation, altruism, serenity, reverence, sacrifice for the good of someone else, etc. In most cases, the specific values of religion overlap with decency and morality. Aesthetic values instill spiritual elevation, sentimental exaltation, an affinity comparable to a religious experience. The paradigm of creative improvisation includes common sense, sanity, a practical vision of the future, etc. In the confines of justice we find ethic responsibility, equity, righteousness, equality, integrity, incorruptibility, etc. These, to a large extent, are encoded in laws and constitutions. The didactogenesis of science stands on the criteria of validity and reliability. Science is the predominant paradigm in the modern world.. It has brought us to the era of informatic ethnogenesis in which we are beginning to live dangerously.

Ethnogenesis is the "cup of life," from where people take the meaning of life, as expressed in the beautiful metaphor of a Cavador Indian, quoted by Ruth Benedict, in the classic, *Patterns of Culture*. The broken cup, meant by the Cavador Indian, is ethonocide. Loss of the ethnogenic fountain source is loss of identity of the planet's pariahs. Every person "drinks in the cup of life of culture," to use Ramon's metaphor, in a particular way. Culture is not a strait jacket. Each person acquires his/her culture in a particular manner called idiosyncrasy. These particularities of individuals are distributed in a normal curve. Those whose performance attains excellence are at the apex of that curve. In the middle, the "normal," conforms to the parameters of values and ideologies, without much' rocking of the boat.' The lower part of the curve contains the low performers and deviants in multiple forms.

Idiosyncrasy in language appears in the form, idiolects. There are as many idiolects as there are particular individuals. Idiolects derive from the epistemic foundation of dialects. When the speakers of a dialect are no longer understood by the speakers of another dialect, as was the case of Spanish, French, Portuguese, Italian and Rumanian, all which were dialects of Latin, they ceased being dialects and became languages. There are people who mistakenly use the word 'dialect' as an inferior form of speech. The fact is that everyone who speaks, speaks an idiolect derived form a dialect. Spain has Andalusians, Galicians, Castilians, Catalonians. Catalonian is regarded a language by linguists. The linguistic affiliation of Basque is unknown. Latin American dialects differ from one country to another and inside each country by regional differences. The moment a 'Cachaco' from Bogota opens his /her mouth, a 'Paisa' from Antioquia has his /her place of origin fixed. In the same way, a 'Pastuzo' (from Pasto) or a 'Costeño' from Barranquilla will identify the place of origin of his fellow countrymen by the dialect of Colombian Spanish they speak. In Argentina, a 'Porteño' may have as much difficulty understanding a Cordovan, as a New Englander in the United States, trying to understand a speaker with a "heavy" Mississippi "accent". Accent, by the way, is a speech difference that characterizes non native speakers. In other words, only foreigners can have an accent.

It is true, as Chomski has argued, that the capacity that

permits us to acquire the most precious gift of language, is innate. The same could be said of the capacity to acquire the most precious gift of the entire culture. Chomski, for sure, would not argue that human flesh and bone are enough for the attainment of the human condition. The specific language we acquire, as well as the epistemic foundation of cognition upon which perception and action is informed at a collective level, is obtained in the learning environment of a culture, not in the genes. Of course, the ability to master the ethnogenic source is distributed in a normal curve. We shall be arguing ahead with the Venezuelan educator Luis Alberto Machado that intelligence is the most violated of all human rights.

The concept of culture has been the foundation of the academic discipline of anthropology. Today, it is also part of disciplines like psychology, sociology and political science. Ethnology has been a rich source of information in the formulation of psycho analytic theory. Culture has been defined as the proverbial pact between the living, the dead, and those yet to be born, a pact to sustain and improve heritage. Human attributes, acquired in the process of enculturation, constitute a way of seeing. The way of seeing informs the way of acting. A child of American parents, raised by adoptive Chinese parents, will not understand a shred of English. If the didactogenesis was Chinese, as in the case of Joseph Rhinehart, his human formation, his perceptions, and his actions for self actualization would be Chinese (See Clyde Kluhkhon, *Personality and Nature, Society and Culture,*(1957.)

The children of Russian, Italian, Puerto Rican, etc. immigrants in the United States may learn to speak English in a way that Wallace Lambert has designated as subtractive. This subtraction discards the language of their parents not because they have a faulty genetic inheritance. If language were a matter of heredity, subtractive acquisition would be impossible. If genes were the source of culture, it would be impossible to understand profound changes in primitive societies who ascend to modernity in a brief period of time. Neither would immigrants acquire the cultural skills necessary to insert themselves in an adoptive culture.

Race is a concept that serves a valid purpose in classifying animals because these inherit their behavior. The spiders of today are the same spiders of millions of years ago. Their conduct emanates from genetic programming. They do not have conceptual representations in the mind of what is ahead and will become reality.. Choice, innovation or creation, are possible because of representation.

A spider," says Marx, "executes operations that emanate from a genetic programming that are similar to the manipulations of the knitter. There is something in the worst master of works that puts the knitter ahead of the bee, by first executing the construction in his brain. At the end of the work process, a result bursts forth, that was in the mind of the worker. Before the beginning of the process, it had an ideal existence." That ideal existence in the mind is the project, the vehicle driving from preexistence, going to a station called, 'existence'in which that which had an ideal existence," becomes reality.

Today, the formula of empowerment should include not just sharing the "piece of the pie", but also the awareness of the fact that when everyday decisional processes are conceived on the foundation of values, the way of seeing and acting warrants human dignity. It is not utopic to speak of human improvement by means of an enculturation where there is awareness of values and of decisional processes that stand on a foundation of values.. To dignify the human condition is a possibility within reach of those who manage the collective decisional processes, especially in the field of education. The concept of culture is of great importance in the planning education for the good life dreamed by all the people of good will on the planet. We plant the seed for the good harvest. Patsy appears, saying that morals can not be legislated. Are not the codes of law the foundation of prescribed or proscribed action in society? What is right is prescribed and what is wrong is proscribed in codes of law, for example the United Nations conventions.

New generations benefit from the correct choices of the past as well as from errors that have been seen as errors. George Santayana said that "he who does not recognize errors from the past is likely to repeat them." He or she who commits unethical actions will use his/her intelligence to find justifications. A repetition compulsion, aimed at justification of inhumanity, threatens life in the planet. If the epistemic foundation of culture is ideology, life becomes (la vida loca). the crazy life, la jueyera as in, *Requiem Para una Cultura.*

A Labyrinth of Solitude, as foreseen by Octavio Paz,.is an existential absurdity as proclaimed by existentialists. There is unanimity in the fact that values are eroded and that the erosion of values is the cause of the increasing rates of criminality, and now wars, in the lumpenized society. What is not usually recognized is that values are part of culture and crisis in value is a crisis in culture.

The government television station presents pop psychologists wearing the hats of sexologists, exposing an erotomanic creed, such as giving advise on coital positions, size of organs, and places where a woman's vagina is most sensitive. There is no effort to discuss love as humanity's highest value. An instrument, such as television, with such humanizing possibilities, becomes an agent of ideology eroding the ethical foundation of the social system. In the world we live in, the value of decency walks head on against vulgarity, especially on television. Whoever dares to assert a preference for morality, as a foundation in human affairs, is deemed a fundamentalist ; a sort of fanatic. What else but fundamentalists are we human beings? The epistemic foundations are fundamentals in the mind that serve to discern and create reality.. These fundamentals may be values, or on the contrary, ideologies. The only other alternative to fundamentalism is S-R automaticities, characteristic of animals and of the lumpenized sectors of a society. (c.f. of the author, *Lumpenizacion,*Rio Piedras, Bayoan, 1992) The lumpen condition is a kind of inhumanity covering the whole planet.

"Words are the instrument of thinking, said Vigotski. The Institute of Puerto Rican Culture is an institution created for the purpose of safe guarding the data bank of the culture of Puerto Rico. "Culture," for the regents of that institution, is reduced to the cosmetic domain of aesthetics. This way they avoid any friction with the interest groups in the establishment who would not want people to be aware of the difference between values and ideologies, or of Aristotle's dictum: "What a society honors will be cultivated." The complex existential map with which people construct their every day reality contains far more than cosmetics..The body of shared understandings, the essence of human beings, contains such important constituents, as the political culture and decency, so badly bruised by younger generations. The rest of the domains of the cultural construction of reality are left.. This truncated view of culture contaminates the minds of our children, through the Department of Education..

On television everyday we see programs where trivialities, such as the private lives of prefabricated celebrities, their sexual scandals, and perverse gossip, are transmitted under the rubric of culture. Culture reduced to aesthetics becomes exotica to attract tourism. There is a commonly heard expression, "when they (United States) sneeze, we get pneumonia). A pattern in the culture of the United States, which we have called 'pseudo ethnicity', utilizes bits of aesthetics as identification of so called ethnics. The pseudo-ethnic avails himself of cosmetic aesthetic markers to confirm a continuity of culture long gone in second and third generations. (See the author, *Pseudo-Ethnicity is a Collective Hallucination, in America Indigena* Mexico, 1986).

The Institute of Puerto Rican Culture is, in fact, an Institute of Folklore, Art and History. It assumes responsibility for that part of the data bank of culture relative to the expressive authenticity of our artisans, our musicians and our artists. They support exhibitions of art, festivals of artisan work, etc. This is not bad. It is very good. What is not good is to confuse one domain of the cultural construction of reality; the cosmetic aesthetic domain, with the total body of epistemic foundations. There are epistemic foundations that ennoble existence, and others that debase it. The epistemic foundations of values support human dignity and sustain the higher potentialities of human beings. Ideologies degrade, oppress, deceive, and stupefy. Violence appears in our mist in an explosion analogous to a civil war.

CHAPTER III

Values

I dreamed that life was pleasure. I woke up and
realized that pleasure is to serve. I served and
saw that to serve is happiness.

R. Tagore

Life is a journey in a "river of decisional processes. Every minute in the life of any human being is transit from preexistence to existence in the vehicle of projects. Project is the state of the future, contemplated as a plan in the present. These are as present in ones life as the air we breathe. There is no way out from the river of decisional process, or in Sartre's words, "not deciding is a decision."

Decisional processes of a culture are informed by two different and opposed epistemic foundations. One such epistemic foundation is the source of decisional processes that ennoble existence. We call it the domain of values. Decisional processes, derived from the epistemic foundations of values, leads to the liberation of creative potentialities, the innate ethical condition con substantial with affinity, solidarity, and creative authenticity, in every day relations with the physical and human environment.. The configurations of perception and action, derived from values, dignifies existence, promotes self actualization, liberates the creative potentialities of human beings, and supports respect of human dignity. Values grant respect, dignity, and integrity, empowering human beings with authentic self esteem and self actualization, and in the process generate the euphoria of solidarity, liberating the creative potentialities innate to human beings.

There is a second epistemic domain diametrically opposed to values...The counter value domain that invalidates oneself and others, is known as false conscience or ideology. Ideology produces configurations of perception and action for the purpose of concealing injustice, error, ignorance, irrationality. It contaminates decisional processes with envy, deceit, avarice, fraud, violence, hatred, revenge, degradation, indignity, deceit, depravation, disrespect for human dignity.

In a society in which values are eroded and ideology prevails, as predicted by Thomas Hobbes, people will resort to the most efficient means to obtain their ends. These are fraud, violence, and deceit. Such a society would look a lot like ours, where love no longer is in the heart, perversions are made to appear as liberation, fatalities are produced by violence, and accidents stain the streets of our world daily with blood. People live behind bars to protect themselves from an army of delinquents Desublimation opens Pandora's box with evil propensities of the polymorph perverse of the id. Dr. Erich Fromm spoke of necrofilia as a sort of collective death wish leading to a Hobbesian state in which violence, fraud, and deception, become the "easy" way to attain ends. Thanatos over awes Eros, the life principle..

Human rationality is assailed and drowned by the waves of the ocean of irrationality. Values have been preached for centuries, yet history to this day remains tainted in blood and tears, caused by never ending wars, random violence, fraud, and depravation. Commitment to values requires more than customary forms of education. We have the case of the Secretary of Education in Puerto Rico, in the years 1998 to 2000, who stole millions of dollars belonging to school children. It's difficult to think that he did not know values. The priests accused of sexual abuse no doubt knew the meaning of values. There is something besides didactic instruction determining a commitment to values. The something else is the ego's capacity to neutralize the raw energy that emanates from the satanic store of evil impulse in the unconscious side of the mind.

That something else was explored by Freud. Freud believed that there is a sinister part, a sort of Mr. Hyde, that he called the id, in every person. The id is, as Dr. Clara Thompson, a disciple of Freud has attested, "a cauldron of antisocial seething excitement that knows no values, no good nor evil, no morality "Jose Enrique Rodo, depicted that evil side of human beings as Caliban, compared with Ariel, the spirit of rationality and enlightenment. (c.f. *Ariel*, Montevideo, 1994) Ariel corresponds to the ego, the spirit of light, contrasted with Caliban, the cauldron of antisocial excitement; the source of evil that Freud identified as the "polymorph perverse" of the id.

The control of the id is the triumph of sublimation. Sublimation was the dream of the alchemists of transforming coarse metals into pure gold. Humanity has known sublimation for centuries in all the forms of spiritual life. The intra-psychic alchemy of sublimation creates the gold of intelligence and ethical awareness for decisional processes that enhances life. The alchemy of sublimation, as the source of values, promotes self actualization in authenticity. The concept of authenticity was brought to ethnological thinking by Edward Sapir in his classic, *"Culture Genuine and Spurious"*. Authenticity is possible where evil antisocial energies are transformed into creative energy by means of sublimation. Sublimation is the miracle of renunciation to egotistic individuation in solidarity with fellow human beings. The ego is the spirit of human solidarity, aimed at self actualization within the design of values. Its psychic energy is derived from the neutralization of the psychic energy of the id transforming it into a source of values.

The concept of culture, as the repository of values, is of great importance if our choice is to plant the seed for the good ethnogenic harvest. Self actualization, in optimal conditions, brings about the creative potentials of human beings. There are destinies in the river of decisional processes that debase the dignity of human beings. as well as the environment, social and natural. Projects derived from values enlighten existence. Planning is intrinsic to human existence. Barbara Wooton deemed planning as oppression. Certainly those with decisional power, if allowed, may plan for oppression. Planning, like freedom, can be used for good or for bad. What is not possible, is not to plan. Options are ever present. Not to plan, to paraphrase Sartre, is to plan the proverbial "flooded river advantage of fishermen." (Rio revuelto ventaja para pescadores). Those who advocate against planning are planners of irrespon-sibility.. Wickedness, violence, and deceit, have brought upon humanity moments of darkness, pain, destruction, and sadness.

Some years ago a psychopath desensitized the authenticity of the people in Germany. Spiritual authenticity declined, while the rivers of decisional processes became rivers of blood, sweat and tears, as stated by Prime Minister Winston Churchill. The world was engulfed in a nightmare of darkness, death, and desolation. The highest degree of brutalization and dehumanization, in our times so far, occurred in the Nazi concentration camps. They are landmarks of tragedy and death, the clearest cases of lack of authenticity. Buchenwald, Dachau, and many others, are names that sadden humanity's conscience. In Nazi concentration camps, human dignity was stepped upon in every possible way. Fear, indignity, fatigue, pain, famine, and finally death in gas chambers, are parameters of existence comparable to Dante's Inferno…Hunger, cold, exhaustion, and finally death by asphyxiation, in chambers of lethal gas, was a via dolorosa traveled every day by inmates in these camps…Forty million lives were lost in Europe alone, with the profound pain and desolation brought to the lives of those left behind. Nazi concentration camps, overseen by sadists, who tortured and killed six millions human beings assumed members of the Hebrew religion.

A religion is not a race. Ideology declared it a race A genocide hardly ever known in history was put in action. Dr. Victor Frankl survived in that reign of terror where six millions of his people succumbed a nightmare populated with sadistic psychopaths. The miracle of his survival validates his theory of logotheraphy. The miracle of Dr. Victor Frankl's survival is the fulfillment of that kind of understanding that many centuries in the past Greek philosophy conceived as logos, the source of authenticity that ancient philosophy conceived as "the verb," purest of all knowledge,. the source of intelligence. Logos signify knowledge, mind, intelligence, comprehension, (Webster, Unabridged, 1977, Pg. 1225.) Logos is the illumination immanent to the true heirs of Prometheus, bearer of authenticity.

Psychoanalysis is epistemology of emotions. Epistemology is the study of the foundations of cognition. Psychoanalysis is a special kind of education that promotes rationality, transparent intelligence and ethical awareness. The high emotional tone, called happiness, is beyond the entrance door of the temple of Delfos, in which there was an inscription, "know thyself." "To thyself be true," has its complement in the "Thou shall know the truth and the truth shall make you free" of Christianity.

Authenticity must be released from the Kafkian domiciliary arrest called alienation, with a return to creative enthusiasm, serenity, and that high level of emotional intelligence, called happiness.. From aberrated premises emerges the irrational action known as 'acting out' (see Chapter IX).

Those emotions that arise from catastrophic sources in the unconscious, produce what H.S. Sullivan called, 'malevolent transformation'. Insight is the light that dissipates the obscurity of those catastrophic residues in the mind. Anthony Mello uses the term, "illumination," for this primordial authenticity. Dr. Frankl survived a nightmare infected with the virus of sadism, that Freud called, 'death instinct' and Fromm called, 'necrophilia'. His survival was possible in a world of iniquity and infamy because he kept his mental set up placed on "a task to be done, a person that waits for one, a commitment that should be complied with." "That is the lesson I had to learn in three years in Dachau and Auschwitz."

Dr. Frankl wanted to offer to humanity what he had learned in that night of terror instituted by Fascists. Logo-therapy intends to attain the restoration of an ethical principle expressed in the previously mentioned proverb, "You shall know the truth and the truth will make you free." In religion, the ethical condition is restored by confession. 'Confession,' in Freudian terms, is the closest possible duplicate of that which in the past constituted a catastrophic event leaving a epistemic turbulence in the mind. Catharsis is a Greek word meaning 'cleansing', in this case the epistemic turbulence left by traumatic experiences or unethical acts. The person is rescued from living a life in Hell at that moment in which exposure of the event releases the traumatic contents. At that moment, a humanistic coef-ficient returns, infused with authenticity, and happiness. On the face of the person liberated from the evil forces of the polymorph perverse of the id, appears a radiance of authenticity, a pure version of happiness. Our Eugenio Maria de Hostos knew ethical happiness and postulated it as immanent to human nature.

Great teachers of humanity, Lao Tse, Buddha, Socrates, Jesus, Hostos, and many others, lived the highest ethic conditions in love, creativity, and harmonious affinity. The happiness ingrained in ethical paradigms has been postulated as immanent to human nature. Sublimation is the miracle of the loaves of bread and fish for a spiritually starved humanity lacking values. Human beings seek happiness in pleasure, but there is a difference between pleasure that becomes distasteful past the immediate moment it is enjoyed. The pleasure of authenticity lasts and transcends in the excellence of euphoria, love, and solidarity that ennobles existence.

John Stuart Mills, criticizing pleasure in hedonism compared with the pleasure of authenticity said, "It is better to be an unsatisfied Socrates than to be a satisfied hog." The option supported in values exalts existence even if the price is sacrifice or loss of life. Emotional intelligence is the highest value. The term 'emotional intelligence' emphasizes the enveloping didactogenic environment composed of the epistemic domains of culture, steering away from the notion of an organic determinism implicit in the term mental health. It emphasizes the enveloping didactogenic environment composed of the epistemic domain of culture. Mental health, defined as a psychology of adjustment stemming from S-R robotical automaticity, is alien to value commitments. Emotional Intelligence is the spiritual serenity attained by bringing into awareness, pain, loss, disappointment, resentment, anguish, despair, anger, and hate, imprinted in the epistemic record. The epistemic windows, through which one looks at the world, must be dispelled of residues from the past, of pain, disappointment, resentment, anguish, despair, hate, and the anger that brings misery in the life of self and people around us. Where the shadows caused by aberrant epistemic foundations are dispelled, enlightenment is recovered. It is as if one awakes from a nightmare. The shadows of irrationality disappear and in their place appears the intrinsic ethical condition. There is unanimity in Puerto Rico on the fact that values are eroded. What is not usually recognized is that values are part of culture, and crisis in value is an ethnogenic crisis. (See the author, *Requiem Para Una Cultura*, Bayoan 1970.

Emotional intelligence is the supreme value; the Tao towards a pristine ethical condition. At the moment the incubus of unconscious disturbances are extinguished there is an illumination in which the pain, the anguish, the desperation, the chaos, and the violence, stamped in psychic windows, are no longer there to disturb life. Where the collective decisional processes and the means of social indoctrination (didactogenesis) fall in the hands of psychopaths, such as Hitler, Pinochet, Somoza, Papa Doc, Trujillo, and so many other assassins of humanity, authenticity declines, while that which Erich Fromm calls 'necrofilia' and Freud calls, 'instinct of death,' contaminate the river of decisional processes, strangling human values.

The Fascist syndrome that affected Germany has been present in recent military dictatorship in Chile, such as that of General Pinochet, who was brought into power by the CIA. In Africa, at this moment, there are Fascist regimes exterminating defenseless people in villages. The image of babies trying to extract milk from their mother's arid breasts, due to starvation, as well as exhaustion and fear of terrorist armies, reminds us that Fascism is still with us. It seems incongruous to see those who were victims in the past become identified with their aggressors, using tanks like the Israel State, in scorching earth operations, and demolishing homes in Arab villages. Israel portrays a case of identification with the aggressor, the Nazis, who imposed upon them the cruelest of all human conditions.

Moments of darkness imposed by planners of wickedness, violence, and deceit, force human history backward.

What lies ahead is a mystery, at a moment when the United Nations, is disregarded and the world falls back into a repetition of past iniquities. The repetition compulsion of encanallados is an ominous promise for the future. Encanallado is the person who commits an act contrary to values and in an effort to justify his /her evil act, intensifies their hatred by blaming the victim. The attempt to justify the unjustifiable obscures the light of Ariel, the spirit of light. There is no word in English to translate this malevolent transformation, that becomes a way of life when people substitute the pristine nature of the ethical condition and become an encanallado. In losing the condition of authenticity, the person assumes a contra-intentional identity, something like the proverbial, "selling ones soul to the devil."

Dostoyevski viewed, with great clarity, the phenomena of encanallamiento portrayed in the character, Fedor Karamasov, when he said; "One day I asked him why he hated someone." He answered, "He has done nothing to me. I hate him because I have insulted him. Since I insulted him I want to have the pleasure to continue hating him." Encanallamiento is a pattern of revulsion and avoidance created in the mind of the person who commits an unethical act against his/her victim. The presence of the victim acts as an S-R trigger that generates an automatic revulsion and antipathy. This sense of revulsion and antipathy is taken as evidence of the malignancy of the victim, a justification of his/her rancorous act.

The encanallado repeats the mendacity compulsively,

and persistently. The missing transparency produces a break in communication, with a concomitant break down in comprehension. When this break in awareness is assumed, transparency becomes blurred and the malevolent transformation is embodied in ideology. The process of restoration of the ethics condition is confession with catharsis..The unethical acts must be confessed to, in order to bring back the rightful ethical condition.

The return to illumination is called insight with logos in the Freudian theory. "To thyself be true," has an additional complement in the path of des- alienation in Christianity, "Thou shall know the truth and the truth shall set you free." The return to the ethics condition is the return to authenticity by means desalienation. The pristine nature of a human being, the spirit of light, appears when the shadows of irrationality are extinguished. Love, kindness, happiness, beauty, and intelligence, strangled by fear and suffering, can be brought back to life by means of emotional re-education. The recovery of the supreme value of emotional intelligence mentally leads to the liberation of affiliative and creative emotions, which are immanent in each person. This innate Ariel is transparency, without strangeness in affinity and understanding of others.

Abraham Maslow used the term "peak experience" which in fact describes that moment in which Caliban influences are extinguished, and on the face of the person appears a radiance of authenticity, a pure version of happiness. The Jesuit priest, Anthony de Mello, in his book, *Illumination*, (Buenos Aires, Edition Karma, 1992) says that, "Nobody does bad things on purpose or through cold wickedness, for the simple reason that a substantial component of our being, adheres to kindness, happiness, beauty, and the intelligence which is the light of truth. If this substance is drowned by fears, by suffering, the only solution is to remove what hinders." Erasing the strangeness that impairs the flow of communication brings about serenity and transparency. This serenity has been known throughout centuries of humanity, in all forms of spiritual life. The pleasure of self actualization is pleasure that lasts, creates, contributes, transcends, and endures.

Where the neutralization of the primary process fails, then the absurdity that we have called lumpenization prevails in the form of violence, depravation, and corruption. Lumpenization is a free reign of the pleasure principle, a "liberation" of the polymorph perverse in ignorance of the reality principle. In human affairs, the bad currency substitutes the good currency in accord with the Gresham law. Decision making processes alien to values produces the conditions for generalized psychopathy. In Central American, countries like El Salvador, Nicaragua and Peru, have overcrowded prisons with no space available, thus delinquents are left out in the streets where they make life insecure for the rest of the population.

The curse of war is ever present in human history. Today, warlords, as heads of governments, have the power for total destruction of life on the planet. On the same list there is the destruction of the lungs of the planet by the destruction of woodland. Also, the contamination of the environment, the deterioration of the air we need to breathe, the poisoning with chemicals of the underground aquifers.

A populist psychology, at the services of mega Capitalism, in need of consumerism, has vulgarized Freudian theory, promoting a permissive negligence for the gratification of narcissistic and hedonistic urgencies, ignoring the fundamental option of values that elevate human existence. Marcuse called 'repressive tolerance' what Erich Fromm called 'negative freedom' and we have called, 'lumpenization.' Responsible, positive permissiveness, or "positive freedom," takes place in the context dialogic communication (see the author, *Communication Dialogica es Felicidad*, Bayoan 1996.) Transparent communication flows without strangeness, without obstacles, where there is no need to place obscurity in order to hide unethical acts.

Great figures of the intellect, exponents of humanistic socialism, like Albert Einstein, Erich Fromm, Bertrand Russel, Jean Paul Sartre, Pablo Neruda, Gabriel Garcia Marquez, hoped for a stop to dehumanization. The hope was placed in the notion of a new man, to be created in Socialism. The new man would have been the Ariel, derived from the epistemic foundation of values. In the first experiments in Socialism, culture was not seen as a second maternal womb in which people attain their humanity. Instead of seeing culture as didatogenesis, for the creation of a new man, it was deemed as an ideological superstructure, obedient to the mode of production. In the German Ideology, Marx wrote the eleventh thesis on Feuerbach, "Philosophers have interpreted diverse forms of the world, but what proceeds is to transform it." This phrase became a prescription for an anti-intellectual activism without reflection.

This vulgarization of Marxism was called 'mechanistic economicism.' The mechanistic economicists see the culture as a "super structure" that reproduces, in an ideological form, the base of an economic structure. Culture is conceived as a mere ideological reproduction of the mode of production. This ideological superstructure is a screen concealing the interests of the dominant class. Under this paradigm, values 'go down the drain.' How could ideology be identified if it were not for its contrast with values?. With an S-R mode of decision making what came as human creation was the old lumpenized robot.

To be aware of ideology and to indict it is good. What is not good is ignoring that it is the awareness of values what makes possible the indictment of ideology. The moment the Soviet Union was overthrown a wave of corruption and criminality emerged, few times seen in history. A horde of corrupt officials swarmed upon the resources of their country as locust, and in a short period of time they had organized the most efficient and bloody mafia in the world. Once S-R controls were released, Caliban, uncontrolled, made up for lost time. A general voracity surfaced, with gangsterism, drug trade, and the sale of vital technology. In this first experiment of Socialism, the hope of a new man failed.

Frans B. M. De Waal, in an issue of, "Scientific American" magazine, argues that the failure of the first experiment in Socialism was caused by an innate egoistic impulse. There is such innate egoistic impulse in Caliban. There is also the Ariel of human values which an ethnogenic circumstance may make real. In an Agrarian Reform community in Puerto Rico employment was "given" as bribery to purchase electoral support. Hiring was based on membership in the political party in power. (see *Social Change and Personality*; Northwestern University Press, 1965.) Education, health, employment, equal justice, were corrupted by politicians who transformed human rights into political bribery to be cashed in the electoral process. These conditions, without ethics, became a learning environment for the new generation. Communality, founded on values, was maintained until a new generation came of age, in a learning environment, where human rights were degraded by corrupt politicians

Today, we sail on a sea of uncertainty, created by the irrationality of ideologies. Life on this planet is under the threat of nuclear holocaust, contamination of the water of lakes, rivers, and of the subsoil, and by the devastation of forests, that are the lungs of the planet, along with the demographic explosion. There is no development program capable of sustaining the demographic explosion. In the Amazon, thousands of tropical hectares of forest are cut down every day to yield the consumerist abundance needed to keep the system going. The layer of ozone, that protects us from the mortal rays of the sun, is perforated by chemical products and the emission of millions of automobiles. Where once fertile soil existed, now desert lands appear. The sword of Damocles is suspended over the life on this planet. There is evidence of an increase in the temperature, that will cause a melting of the polar ice cap and with it the consequential increase in the rising of the seas, and the disappearance of present coastal areas beneath the water.

For the moment, consumerism is a festival of drugged multitudes. What is not a festival, is social chaos. Eroticism, used for S-R reinforcement, creates a stampede of an erotomanic epidemic. Sex and violence, the two most powerful impulses of Caliban, are used as incentives for consumerism. A ship full of garbage, traveling from port to port, trying to unsuccessfully obtain permission of entry, is a sort of symbolic representation of our times, expressed in Antonio Machado's, "A Donde el Camino Ira." The ghost of wasteful refuse from consumerism has no place to go. Life itself is not valued with the prospect of nuclear war.

CHAPTER IV

Ideology and Human Invalidation
Part I

"God is dead. Everything is permitted."

Dostojevski

The emperor had the desire to wear the most beautiful garment ever seen by human eyes. He contracted the most exquisite couturier with the highest rank and reputation in his reign. The day of the debut arrived. The global television cameras were there to transmit the splendid event. The public flooded the streets, admiring the unusual beauty of the emperor's garment.

Ideology had not stunted the authenticity of perception of a boy watching from the sidelines. He suddenly exclaimed, "The emperor is naked." There was silence and then a rising multitudinous laughter filled all the valleys and mountains of the kingdom. The multitude, with one voice, clamored, "The emperor is naked." Where the "open sesame," with which we open the door to enter the world of reality is ideology, every day decisional processes are contaminated with vices such as the adulation portrayed in this story of the emperor's garment, or, worse than that, with the brutality, sadism, and perversions, that have pervaded the lumpenized world.

The Allegory of the Cavern of Plato represents the first glance into the fallacy of ideological thought. In this metaphor, false conscience is represented by a group of people locked up in a cave. They see the shadows projected on the walls of the cave and think that those shadows are the things themselves. One captive escapes and finds out that his people have been deceived by false conscience. He returns to the cave and tries to explain to his fellow captives that the shadows are not things but reflections on the walls of the cave of things in the world outside. They refuse to believe him and kill him. This statement on ideology was intended as an expose of the execution of Socrates.

The differentiation between representation (in here) and the thing (out there) has been a recurrent subject in the history of ideas. Korsibski used the term, 'map' as representation and 'territory' for that which the map represents. Another great philosopher, Emanuel Kant, made a differentiation between reality and representation. He called the appearance of things, 'phenomenon', and the things in themselves, 'noumeno'. People "see" the representation, and in most cases assume, like Plato's cave dwellers, that the image that is in their sense organs is the thing itself.

John Saxe, in a humorous anecdote, depicts as Hindustani blind men, those who mistakenly assume that the perception in the mind and the thing out there are the same. A convention of blind Hindustani has convened to debate the nature of the elephant of India. The first speaker reaches out and touches the elephant's legs. His verdict is pronounced with unquestionable authority: "The elephant is a temple that elevates its columns to the sky". A second speaker reaches out and touches the belly of the elephant. In exercising his right to dissent he exclaims, "My dear colleague, the elephant is not a temple, it has never been one. The elephant is an immense globe." The next blind speaker touches the tail of the elephant and declares, "The elephant is a cane of bamboo, long and sinuous."

Deepak Chopra writes: "out there you may be seeing a football stadium filled with thousands of people. The real phenomenon is a small electrical impulse inside your brain that you, the non local being, interpret as a football game". (Deepak Chopra, *The Spontaneous Fulfillment of Desire*, New York Harmony Books 2003 p 73).

Alfred North Whitehead called "misplaced concreteness" the naive realism that confuses the representation (in here) with the thing in itself (out there). Another term for the same process is reification. Beyond reification there are hallucinations that lead to the irrationality we shall discuss ahead as 'acting out'. Epistemes at the level of emotions range from the heights of enthusiasm and creativeness, down to the doldrums of apathy and still lower to aberration. (see "Three forms of insertion in decisional processes: acting out, naive realism, critical thinking" in *Educacion Valores, Salud Mental*, Rio Piedras, Bayoan.1989 Piedras,Bayoan,1989).

Epistemes may produce distortions in perception. The confusion of abstraction (in the mind) with the thing in itself (out there) has been the source of much pain and suffering when those who hold the reins of power, impose what they see as dogma, with methods of torture, such as burning at the stake, the way used in the Inquisition and other absolutist regimes. Ideology is the institutionaliza-tion of fallacy. Napoleon conceived ideology as intentional fraud, committed by intellectuals. Geiger asserts that, "All ideology is based on adhesions (associative type S-R auto-maticities),in a paratheoric mode. Karl Mannheim, in his book, *Ideology and Utopia,* attributes the term "ideology" to Francis Bacon. Francis Bacon (1561-1626) expounded a method of falsifying hypothetical epistemic constructs to attain high reliability. That led to the advancements of the scientific revolution, up to present day. He asserted that the perceptive faculty is distorted, at times, by false mirrors that he designated as' idols':

the idols of the tribe,

idols of the cave.

idols of the marketplace

idolatry of the theater

Tribalism appears in street gangs and in intellectual cliques, often referred to as academic mafia, political parties etc., each with a private entrapment of the mind in analogy to the Platonic cave. In the idolatry of the market-place, money talks in the voice of Poderoso Caballero Don Dinero. (Powerful voice is that of Mr. Money).. Idols of the forum and the theater prevail in countries, such as those in our Spanish tradition where rhethoricism, theatrical histrionism, and aesthetic preferences, take priority over and above other values.

The Jesuit priest, Anthony de Mello, wrote in his book, *La Iluminacion,* "Religion, in essence, is liberty, with neither fanaticism nor ideologies. Ideologists have done much harm to religion and continue on that path of deception." For Marx, ideology is an epistemic lens created for the purpose of concealing social injustice in order to safeguard the privileges of the dominant social class. The dominant ideas, in any moment in history, are those that fit the interests of the dominant class,. Their power results from their control of the means of production, which happens to be the means of sustenance of a society. In order to justify the appropriation of the means of production, they assume control of the didactogenic means with which people create the configurations of perception that are reality for them The means of communication, press, radio, television, become didactogenic means to safeguard their interests. Employment opportunities, promotions, status reputations, are managed by their hired gate keepers.

Ideology is an instrument of domination, even more effective than an army or a cadre of torturers. Ideology conceals injustices, errors, the invalidation of creative potentialities, and human dignity. Gate keepers, who own or administer the didactogenic instruments work hard to deceive the masses with false epistemic configurations that interfere with the correct reading of the text of reality. The official falsehood is intended to conceal injustice and to justify infamy. How could a society with a high intellectual tradition like Germany accept a doctrine of racial superiority and commit crimes that outrage the conscience of humanity. A right wing coup d'etat, performed by the military in Venezuela, was presented on the news as a "vacuum of power" left by the President who fled, no less than to Cuba. The golpistas were sort of drawn into the vacuum to take the rudder of an abandoned ship. As it turned out, the coup was defeated and the democratically elected President Chavez regained his position.

A news program on television, keeps the "War on Terror" on top of the screen for an entire hour, intended as an interpretation of the news on the war in Iraq. Never in the press, have I heard or read a reference to the book of Alan M. Dershowitz, *Supreme Injustice*, a commentary on the USA Supreme Court's decision to stop the unfinished re- counting of votes in Florida that conceded electoral triumph to George Bush (Oxford University, Press,2001). Innate immanent justice is thwarted in the minds of the people. This stunting of the mind must have happened to the people of Germany, who allowed crimes to humanity, of a genocidal character. Yellow press prospers. More so, the scandal sheets and pornography.

...Pornography equals in profits the sale of arms and the drug traffic.

The German Sociologist, Max Weber, called Protestant ethics the epistemic paradigm that gave birth to a new class of small entrepreneurs who had taken over history, and have held it since.then. The Feudal world collapsed, confronted with the thrust of this new class It is called "bourgeoisie." The empowerment paradigm of this new class was austerity, sobriety, frugality, laboriousness, thrifti-ness, (a penny saved is a penny earned) temperance, and postponed gratification. Adam Smith was the ideologist of this new system. Talcott Parsons has indicated, that in the paradise of Adam Smith, who was the philosopher of Capi-talism, there was a serpent. That serpent in that paradise had been noticed by Marx in the theory of surplus value.

Surplus value is the difference between the total price of that which is produced and the wages and salaries received by the greater number of workers. Wages and salaries are not sufficient to purchase what is produced, being only a part of the total price of that which is produced. The part of production that is not consumed accumulates. The "law" of supply and demand advises reduction of prices. At some point, such a reduction causes losses leading to closures and bankruptcy. Closures increase unemployment and unemployment reduces the purchasing power of consumers. Goods continue to accumulate. The process may acquire the characteristics of a downward spiral, ending with a collapse of the economy. This is what happened on Black Tuesday, in the year 1929, when the economy collapsed. Marx had made a prediction, "Upon arriving at a specific phase of development, the productive forces would collide with the existing relations of production. A period of social revolution would begin."

The designers of decisional processes were ready to meet the crisis, inventing remedies to keep the system going. The Welfare State benefactor of Capitalism would buy portions of the congested production and distribute it, in Evita Peron style.. In this way, the congestion was alleviated. Public works created employment to restore the purchasing power of consumers. Some of the public works were considered trivial, often portrayed as hiring workers to make a hole in the ground and then paying other workers to refill it. There were other projects which were not so trivial, such as the monumental Tennessee Valley Authority, and the Grand Coulee Dam, (in the State of Washington), the eighth wonder of the world. This powerful hydro electric dam provided energy for the production of ships and other armaments for World War Two. Production in war industries, and the recruitment of the unemployed for the army, restored the power of the economy

Welfare money, unemployment benefits, retirement, recuperates the purchasing power of consumers. Bank deposits, are insured by the Federal government, to prevent depositors from stampeding to withdraw their deposits, like that which occurred on Black Tuesday, 1929, and more recently in Argentina. Social welfare measures are both a social vindication as well as restoration of the purchasing power of consumers.. Stock market shares are made available as well as loans to purchase homes, cars and household appliances. Reduced interest rates on loans facilitate the purchase of homes. Ownership of property tends to make people more conservative. Subsidized quotas control overproduction.

Labor Unions came into the picture in a sort of stick and carrot game to protect workers rights.. An increase in wage was soon nullified by increased prices. Wage increases, fought by organized labor, served as S-R reinforcement. Rewards, spaced between non rewards, produced the strongest possible fixation on a positive state of mind with the expectation of improvement. Labor leaders soon began to live like potentates.

In Puerto Rico, with the triumph of the P.P.D. (Popular Democratic Party), in the early 1940s, the government assumed responsibility for the construction of highways, schools, and hospitals, providing opportunities previously unknown among the poor. The pants given to the poor, by the Puerto Rican Economic Reconstruction Administration, (La Prera) entered the folklore in couplets with music from La Cucaracha:

Los calzones de la Prera
Se conocen donde quiera
Porque no tienen bolsillos
Ni tampoco relojera

The Authority of Electric Energy initiated a process of electrification for those areas lacking this service. With electricity came light, the radio, television, refrigerators, and electric stoves. The Aqueduct Authority brought running water to homes where it was hauled from public springs. The women who had washed on the banks of the ravines, now had electric washing machines in their dwellings. The telephone company followed the development trend, so that now most houses have telephones. Television, internet, and cellular communication networks, cover the island. Roads and credit opened the way to ownership of cars. Today there are so many cars on the road, that there is a bumper to bumper bottleneck from coast to coast, poisoning the environment with motor fumes. The erosion of the ozone layer in the atmosphere follows.

Lenin observed that Imperialism is a stage in which the relative "overproduction" of Capitalism is relieved of its accumulated congestion in the colonial market, while at the same time securing cheap raw materials and cheap labor. In Puerto Rico, Operation Bootstrap created a government agency to entice foreign capital with all kinds of privileges as well as buildings and tax exceptions to entice foreign capital.. This strategy has become a worldwide pattern. Today, Third World countries plead and offer all kinds of incentives to foreign enterprises to come and make investments and create jobs Fighting them off, as Mexico and Argentina did in the past, is out of the question. International finance agencies, such as the Banco Internacional de Desarrollo and El Fondo Monetario Internacional, provide credit and give advise to meet the conditions required by the lending institutions which are usually the privatization of previously nationalized enterprises.

The world, in truth, has become a 'World Village. Today, under the paradigm of transnational mega Capitalism, computer operations, for example, are conducted, to a large extent, in India. Clothing enterprises are located in many Third World countries, in need of jobs for their people. Oceans and mountains and great distances are no obstacle to cyberspace. High technology controls communication and with it the reality construct in the people's minds. For example, it is hard to believe that the beautiful music styles in Latin America, boleros, tangos, rancheras, and folkloric music, have been abandoned by the young people and substituted by U.S.A. styles of music. Satellites travel around the planet, high in the atmosphere, making reality of Orwell's prediction, "Big Brother is watching you." The dream factory of Hollywood has a worldwide impact. Malcolm X was amazed that African audiences cheered the "good" one, the cowboy, who jumps the gun to kill the "bad" ones, the Indians.

The horn of abundance of mega Capitalism needs consumers to avoid accumulation and congestion. The horn of abundance of mega Capitalism clamors for buyers. In the emerging global economy the small and free enterprises, that have broken the backbone of Feudalism, became an anachronic existential paradigm. Small enterprises can not compete against big capital. The budget, for example, of General Electric, and General Motors or any other transnational mega enterprise, is many times over and above the national budget of many Latin American republics.

The epistemic design of liberal Capitalism: austerity, sobriety, frugality, laboriousness, thriftiness, temperance, and postponed gratification, crashed head on against the aims of mega Capitalism, who needed consumerism as air for their lungs. These values, interfere with the creed of consumerism, so they must be abolished. The epistemic foundation of the original free enterprise system must be deleted in the minds of the people, in order that the paradigm of consumerism can move ahead and prosper.

Social engineering technicians were enlisted and financed with government funds, transferred to Universities for the purpose of creating the design for a consumerist society. Vance Packard's book, *The Hidden Persuaders*, (New York; McKay 1957) is an indictment against a social engineering technology instituted by programmers of the mind to promote a way of life, cut to the style of consumerism. Vance Packard, William H. Whyte, Jules Henry, C. Wright Mills, Wilson Bryan Key have all described how the emotional immaturities of the people were studied in order to discover and exploit them. Great sums of money were made available by the government to universities for motivation research. One of the important considerations for a candidate to be accepted to a position in a University is "grantmanship" an expertise to obtain public funds.

The work ethics interferes with immoderate spending in consumer goods..It must be deleted from the epistemic foundations of people. A school of pop psychology emerged to promote irresponsible permissiveness, aimed at removing inhibitions that interfere with desires that, in the last analyses, end up in the market as purchasing desires. The term "workaholic," an analogy to 'alcoholics', debunks laboriousness. A circle of hidden persuaders, witchcraft apprentices, boosted the polymorph perverse of the id, whose single fixed purpose is satiation of hedonistic pleasures and narcissistic impulses. The hidden persuaders, in the hats of pop psychologists, institutionalized the new freedom, proclaiming sexual liberation as a necessary condition for mental health. Sexual inhibition, deemed as the cause mental disturbances, was to be avoided.

The Freudian postulate of love and work, within the scope of the reality principle, was turned around, placing love in the genitals to promote the pleasure principle, in disregard for the reality principle. Raw sexuality then stood as criteria of normality, nullifying Freud's definition of normality of love and work. The term "genitality," used by Freud, was unfortunate. Freud used the term, 'genital" in reference to the highest stage of human maturation. A vulgarization of Freudian theory contrived genitality as mere genital excretion. Authentic love, as an option that ennobled existence, was deemed romantic and old fash- ioned.. Love appears in old movies filmed before coital scenes made their appearance, and vulgarity invaded the spectacle. Love, in the permissive paradigm, is no longer in the heart, but in the genitals.

Freud compared the ego to a man on an untamed horse, in danger of being thrown out of control by the brutal strength of the animal. Sex is a powerful giant. The ego transforms the crude impulses of the id's polymorphic perversions by means of neutralization and sublimation. Its powerful energy is transformed into the most beautiful and creative of all human possibilities, in the alchemy of sublimation.. In that transformation, the first principle of psychoanalysis, "where the id was, the ego will be" is accomplished. The process of neutralization transforms hedonistic impulses into the rational control, leading to humanization. This is the triumph of the ego over the perversions of the id. The id has a single fixed purpose, a satiation of hedonistic pleasures and narcissistic impulses., Dr. Clara Thompson diagnosed the id as: "a chaos, a cauldron of seething excitement, where there is nothing corresponding to the idea of time. The id knows no values, no good and evil, no morality."

As we have already mentioned, sublimation was the dream of ancient alchemists to transform crude metals into gold. The crude metals, in these cases, were the primitive impulses of the polymorphous perverse of the id, which were transformed into values. In sublimation, crude energies of the id become fuel for creative work. The rationality of the ego is under constant siege by the evil and irrational forces of the id. The equilibrium of the ego depends on its capacity to neutralize the raw energy that emanates from the id. The ego neutralizes the id's hedonistic impulses, and distills them into creative energy. The neutralization of the primary process is necessary for humanization.

Desublimation brings humanity to one of the most violent and perverse moments in history..Desublimation is an unleashing of coarse impulses contained in the Pandora box., the ancient metaphor in reference to the id. In desublimation "the barbarians," that besiege ethic fortress of the ego, tear off its defenses, spreading insanity, hatred, necrofilia, misanthropy, violence, addiction, depravation, crudeness, erotomania and obscenity, over the face of the earth. The erosion of values threatens the peace, the security, and the existential stability of the contemporary world..

Vulgarity and profanity, involving both sex and violence, bring into the every day life of mass society, an epidemic of violence, deaths in accidents, drugs, armed robberies, and rape. Negligent permissive upbringing leads to a Lord of the Flies condition. Lord of the Flies is a story of a group of children shipwrecked on an uninhabited island in the Pacific. There is a gradual process of erosion of social control, progressively crossing the threshold into a Hobbesian condition. Violence prevails. The strong establish their domination over the weak and end up murdering them as a pastime.

Lord of the Flies is, nowadays, a reality in places like the Columbine school in Colorado, where two teenage students massacred one of their teachers and killed and wounded fellow students. Lord of the Flies is today a reality in a world where children are members of organized gangs who fight in the streets. In Bogota, Colombia, they are used as sicarios (hit men) by the mafia. M. Scott Peck, in his book, *The Road Less Traveled*, attests to the permissive ethics produced by the vulgarization of Freudian theory. "You may remember that forty years ago when Freud's theories first filtered down to the intelligentsia and were misinterpreted, as it often happens, there were a bunch of avant garde parents who, having learned that guilt feelings could have something to do with neurosis, resolved that they were going to raise guilt free children. What an awful thing to do to a child. Our jails are filled with people who are there precisely because they do not have any guilt. We need a certain amount of guilt in order to exist in society."

Fundamental human rights, conquered with the heroic sacrifice of previous generations, are blamed for the mishaps of the desublimation caused by the permissive irresponsible so called liberation. When sublimation fails desublimation brings forth the destructive components of Pandora's box, the powerful forces of the polymorph perverse, the evil forces of hatred, that Freud called the id. Not to frustrate her oedipal son, mother Yocasta should have sexual intimacy with her son. Degradation and perversion, insanity, hatred, necrofilia, violence, addiction, erotomania, misanthropy, depravations, procacity, crudeness, obscenity, spread around the whole planet, as if the Greek myth of the Pandora Box were a prophecy of our times. All property is in danger of plunder. The kingdom of terror contaminates the human environment with violence, distrust and insensitivity. An army of mercenaries force the people to live behind iron bars.

The natural environment is gradually degraded. Subterranean waters are contaminated. Rivers have been converted into sewers, an example being the Tequendama River in Bogota, which is one of the worst. Our air is poisoned with emissions of gas fumes from the millions of automobiles. The hot house effect, produced by the erosion of the ozone layer, seems like a sword of Damocles, suspended above humanity's neck, threatening life on the planet. An increase in temperature is bringing about a melting of the polar caps, followed by the rising waters of the seas and the disappearance of the lowlands, being submerged beneath the water.

The discovery of the unconscious, by Sigmund Freud,

might have been a great design for the improvement of the quality of human life. This is a case like that of the surgeon's scalpel in the hands of an assassin. A vulgarized version of Freud's theory has been used as justification for an irrational, convulsive, discordant, irreverent and irresponsible style of life produced by desublimation. This style acquired a philosophical reputation in pop existentialism. Years later it became the style of the Hippies. Unconditional indulgence and idleness result in over satiation and boredom, in the style of Roman bacchanals.

A case illustrating the drama of over satiation and boredom is that of Howard Hughes. Howard Hughes squandered his existence in alcoholism, sex, and uprooted traveling. His life ended in complete isolation and despair, his going from one continent to another in search of something which he never found, a "fever" which was "not in the covers", as is said in the folk maxim, 'The fever,' was in his mind. Another famous victim of empty meaninglessness is the heiress of the Woolworth stores. The paradise promised by hedonism is indeed a road to an existential void.. An existential void, becomes a barrel without a bottom. The proverbial, "poor millionaire," lives the proverbial empty meaninglessness in the ordeal of Tantalus. He/she possess the treasures of the world, but do not own anything, as if he /she were a vagrant.

In the learning environment, of the lumpen society, frustration is to be avoided in all forms and manner while hedonistic permissiveness and negligent irresponsibility prevail.. A so called 'sexual liberation' proclaims sexual promiscuity and an impudent style of life, doing away with modesty.

The creed that mental stress is a product of sexual frustration is disseminated to a point in that a lady psychologist, on the government television station that is supposed to provide educational material, advocates the sex act as a remedy for stress. An erotomanic epidemic yields the bitter fruit of forty per cent of all births from girls still in early childhood.. Children bringing up children.

In a desublimated world all the evil impulses contained in the unconscious spread over the face of the earth by means of what Marcuse called, 'repressive tolerance' and Erich Fromm called, 'negative freedom.' Marcuse, in his classic, *Eros and Civilization:* argues that "The uncontrolled Eros is as fatal as its deadly counterpart, the death instinct." In *Civilization and its Discontents,* Freud argued that "Where civilization fails, man becomes a savage beast, alien to any consideration to protect the lives of his fellow man. "

Consumerism attempts to fill an existential void, in a 'barrel without a bottom' type of existence. Existential emptiness drives people to the shelves of supermarkets. Over consumption ends up in garbage dumps

In the Third World, impoverished sectors live by collecting this garbage.

The erosion of values, brings into reality Dostojevski's lament, "God is dead, everything is permitted."

CHAPTER V

Ideology and Human Invalidation
Part II

Someone asked Freud for a definition of normality
His answer was, "A person who loves and works."
A somewhat similar answer was given by Marx, when he said,
"The alienated person avoids work as if it were the plague."

Pogrammers of collective didactogenesis learned, from the behaviorist psychology experiments with rats, that a pleasure stimulus, placed in contiguity to a neutral stimulus, (for example a bell and the food) pervades and permeates the neutral stimulus. The bell in Pavlov's experiments was a neutral stimuli until paired with food a number of times

The pleasure response provoked by food was transferred to the sound of the bell. Social scientists, of the highest technical caliber, with an S-R technology, apply that formula to allure consumers A beautiful women, in scanty clothing, is placed next to a market product. Appetites that belong to the beautiful women in erotic poses are transferred to products by S-R associative contagion. In every day television audience see such images of eroticism in contiguity to products in the market. In the commercial for soap, a lot more space is given to the attractive young woman in the bathtub than to the product itself. The erotic enchantment of semi dressed beauties, sort of rubs their attractiveness in the product. An attraction, that in fact belongs to the beautiful woman, is transferred to the product.

Candidates for public positions are advertised in the same way.

S-R push button simplicity, in political campaigns, substitutes discernment about the program presented by candidates. The Marxist prophecy that "the price will be confused with the value "becomes reality in today's world since "the image is the thing." The Platonic cave is resurrected.

Millions of dollars are spent in electoral campaigns designed by professional image builders. In this world, phantasmagorias things, that have nothing to do with one another, when "paired" by didactogenic manipulators, are then conceived as causally related, sort of paired in the mind. The learning environment, (didactogenesis) created through the S-R push button style, allows little space to the conceptual thinking. Without conceptual thinking, reality testing fades and anti intellectualism is the rule. Where sublimation fails, persons are exposed to the destructive components of the unconscious mind. The magnitude of the unconscious in human personality is, according to Freud, comparable to the nine tenths part of an iceberg under the water. The programmers of desublimation are aware of the power of the id over the ego. They have at hand the advantages of publicity machinery never before known in history.

A world of associative S-R implants produces an irrational mode of thinking. Analogy is confused with homology. This ideological didactogenesis produces a life style we have called, lumpenization. Lumpenization is a result of the erosion of conceptual thought, and its substitution by S-R cartoon like mentality,. Lumpen is a term employed by European sociologists to describe the alienation from the epistemic foundation of values produced by extreme poverty. Oscar Lewis called it, "culture of poverty." Andre Gunder Frank applies the term, "lumpen bourgeoisie," to the spiritual impoverishment of the opulent sector of society that has lost the capacity for conceptual thinking. The lumpen bourgeoisie live in spiritual poverty, in the mires of human indignity, on the road of desublimation and reification.

Lumpen is a wind vane moved by S-R repulsion attraction,- a robot programmed by S-R triggers in the environment. In the lumpen world, the pleasure principle prevails over and above the reality principle. The unawareness of the epistemic foundations of perception, inhabit our world with robots, prophesied by H.G. Wells, in his novel, *The Time Machine.*

Lumpen is a sort of "pleasure" addict, alien to all ethical consideration, in a world of material incentives, 'loyal' to whomever can provide material provisions. Alien to all ethical consideration, lumpen follows whosoever has ownership and power to distribute S-R incentives.

An English philosopher of the XVI century, Thomas Hobbes, prophesied, in a way, what today we would call lumpenization. Hobbes said that where the ethical bases of a society (civil society) are eroded, the people will resort to the most expedient methods to attain their purposes, which are deceit, fraud, and violence. Life in such a society would become brutalized, horrendous, and brief. A Hobbesian kind of state exists in sectors of societies whose existence is pervaded with prostitutes, perverts, and degenerates.

In many metropolises of Central America., there are areas that resemble a war zone, embattled by gangs who fight one another to control the sale of drugs. These areas live on the edge of the Hobbesian state, without ethical controls, with rampant crime, corruption, destructiveness, perversions, and larceny. In many cases, the police and other officials of justice, are corrupted. In Mexico, institutionalized corruption of the police is known as "mordida." Incorruptible judges, and higher ups, such as the Minister of Justice of Colombia, Rodrigo Lara Bonilla, have faced death at the hands of narco gangsters.

The lumpen world is a sort of celebration of the satanic forces of the id, polluting the planet with erotomania, insanity, necrofilia, misanthropy, addictions, depravations, hate, rapacity, crudeness, obscenity, envy, violence, deceit, degradation, indignity, and depersonalization. There are few places on the planet where the deep structure of value paradigms has not been eroded and substituted by lumpenization. Conceptual critical thinking becomes old fashioned, and intellectuals are dealt with as the new square pegs in the round holes of the system. (see *Lumpenization*, Rio Piedras, Bayoan 1993)

Lumpenization is to a society what psychopathy is to individuals. Anti social propensities make a presence in the violence of wars, eternally present in humanity. Hitler, Torquemada, Mason, Genghis Khan, Tamerlane, the Reverend Jones in Guyana, the Klu Klux Klan, among many others, are personifications of the evil component in human nature.

The German society, with a rich cultural tradition, was drawn into the worst crimes against humanity, under the power of a demagogue capable of eroding their values. Germany, under Hitler, must have lived a loss of values, the same as dehumanization.. Much is to be feared, that something likewise might happen in the United States, of late violating fundamental human rights. Padilla was arrested with no legal assistance, no bail, no just and rapid trial.. (see William Blum, *The Rogue State,* (Common Courage Press, 2000).

Violence appears in our mist in an explosion analogous to a civil war. Dr. Erich Fromm spoke of necrofilia as a sort of collective death wish, leading to a Hobbesian state, in which violence, fraud and deception become the "easy" means to attain ends. Thanatos contrasts with Eros. The life principle leading to authenticity is indeed a vicissitude. Crowds of young girls shout lubric screams and tear off the clothes of celebrities for souvenirs in a collective hysteria.. Provoking sexual appetites, to entice consumerism, require mass production of celebrities. The programmers of collective didactogenesis manufacture the luxuriant additive of celebrities to rub in their lubricity on the product, by S-R contiguity.. They are the role models for our youth. These days, girls show their midriffs, and in many cases are tattooed the way many jail birds are. Manufactured celebrities are maintained in the eyes of the public, on television, in magazines, and in all possible every day programs labeled culture.. There are magazines which acclaim goddesses of the erotomanic cult these fabricated celebrities. An accomplice to this fabrication is the paparazzi who pursue the fabricated celebrities and besiege them, promoting a measure of their importance.

Sex is hot merchandise in commercial propaganda, with lubricity as an attraction.. On the pages of one of the magazines for ladies, one can find prescriptions for timid girls whose shyness impedes them from enjoying an orgasm. Playboy sells millions of copies of an edition containing a naked picture of Marilyn Monroe. "Lady Chatterley's Lover" sold six million copies in one year. The genitals are conceived as the center of the universe, the door to an earthly paradise in the ideology of hedonistic permissiveness

The talents of some singers is not in knowing how to sing, but in revealing, if a woman, naked hips or bursting bosoms with sexually suggestive movements. For a man, the trick is to make lewd gestures, imitating Elvis Presley. "No longer is it necessary to have a good voice," predicted a popular song before television had arrived. The song said, "the television will soon arrive." It was an exact prediction. Today, the roller coaster is down to a musical style where percussion accompanies profanities.

The magic of S-R push bottom simplicity transmutes trivialities into wonders. Existential emptiness drives people to the shelves of supermarkets, or into any bed for casual sex, and in extreme cases to the escape from reality in drugs.

Pop psycho- therapists advise going on a trip, starting

a love affair, buying a new car, a new house, or buying new clothes. Buy, Buy, Buy, is the core axiom of repressive tolerance since it is tailored to the needs of the system to promote consumerism. The wealthy classes of Latin America are heirs to a tradition of ostentation and wasteful expenditure. The riches of the New World were squandered, going into the coffers of early Capitalists in Protestant Europe. In those countries, where thriftiness raises the stigma of stinginess, prevails laziness, ostentation, extravagance, waste, luxuriousness, vanity and the paradigm of consumerism, "lock, stock and barrel," by the leisure class.

The consumerist style of life is nothing new in Latin America. The riches of Venezuelan oil have brought fat coffers to the merchants in Miami. The riches of Argentina, in the decade of the forties, did not give fruit. Today, Argentina is one of the poor houses of the world. Consumerism requires astronomical national debts that become a mortgage of the future. This is the heritage that we leave for forthcoming generations, in addition to the model of character formation, cut to the size of Malinche. In government, corruption is epidemic. The Argentinean Socialist, Eduardo Galeano, calls this leisure class, 'proxenetas' (pimps), in his classic, *Por las Venas Abiertas del Continente*. (Mexico,Era, 1971). These proxenetas (pimps) are promoters of an existential uprootedness of malinchismo, mimetizing styles of music, from the center of Globalized didactogenesis.

The illusive notion of remedying the existential void with material objects, in fact increases meaninglessness and ends up in boredom. The expected enjoyment fades away like Tantalo who intended to quench his thirst, but the moment he neared the water it moved away.. The unquenched thirst for things is felt as depression. Depression is loss. Reaching out on the open shelves in the stores, a multitude of buyers live the ordeal of Tantalus. The objects are discarded. The result is the accumulation of tons of useless items.

Underprivileged children, in the capitals of the Third World, become scavengers in the mountains of wasted goods from consumerism, a world tragedy that most people prefer to ignore. There is a story of a poor million-aire suffering the despair of Tantalus. He is advised to wear the shirt of a happy man to remedy his own misery. He searches everywhere, and at last finds the happy man.. To his surprise, 'the happy man' has no shirt. Many idols, created by promoters of the crazy life style, seek drugs as an illusive remedy for their existential void. Sleeping with multiple mates only deepens the void.

Eric Berne formulated a diagnostic category called Patsy. Patsy is a woman who is so absolutely "good" that she brings the bottle to the alcoholic, in the same way the Mickey Mouse professor concedes good grades in Chinchales. Who would question Patsy's irresistible sweet-ness? She only wants people to have fun. What if they die of cirrhosis, or cause death on the highways? Patsy, in the school system of today, distributes condoms to the chil-dren, in a personification of permissiveness. Patsy's good intentions in government programs generate indolence, the mother of all vices. By giving away the fish, the opportunity to teach people how to fish is lost. Handouts produce a sort of professionalization of mendacity.

In the history of Puerto Rico, Patsy promoted the 3-B government with Baile (dancing),Botella (bottle), and Baraja (cards for gambling). This style was implanted by Governor La Torre at the time when Latin American countries were in rebellion against Spanish domination. His slogan was, "people that have fun will not conspire." Nicolas Maquiavelo, in his infamous work, *El Principe*, advised Cesar Borgia to use the S-R formula—-adulation and bribery, and if that did not work, the iron fist was next on the agenda to maintain power.

Witchcraft apprentices, graduates from pop psychology, enter institutions in the guise of sexologists, to promote a cheap version of love. Sex is presented as the cure, to the old wine in new bottle, called stress. A fanciful genital stage is sought after by means of casual sex, not in love and work as Freud had proposed. Psychotherapy became a school for promiscuity.

A vulgarized version of psychoanalysis conceived orgasm as the philosophical stone that solves all problems. Wilhelm Reich, with a distinguished career, was drawn into the erotomanic crest. He provided his patients with an orgone box to capture a supposed orgasmic energy, free floating in the atmosphere. Timothy Leary, a psychologist, at Harvard University, showed in the beginning of his career the promise of professional excellence. Absorbed by the hedonist stampede, he ended up prescribing the use of drugs, the worst of them, LSD. His doctrine conceives life as a drug trip. It denies the responsibility immanent to life in society, and conceives the existence as a permanent orgy. Margaret Mead, in publications about primitive communities, published, in the category of scientific ethnology, a description of a community where sexual licentiousness was the cause of a supposed paradisiacal happiness. *Love Under the Palm Trees,* expressed lyrically, 'that'lustful happiness. Follow up studies have shown that there was no such licentiousness in the islands of the Pacific. (cf Freeman, Derek, *Margaret Mead and Samoa :The Making and Unmaking of an Anthropological Myth,* Harvard Press, 1983.) Neither was there supposed Rousseaunian happiness among the inhabitants of those islands.

Magical solutions prosper, while values are substituted by ideologies. Ideology, is false consciousness. The pleasure that emanates in creation, generosity, and all values, remains unrecognized. The lumpen world came forth with deviations and perversions in a Roman kind of existential bacchanal. Television bombards audiences with raw images of sex and violence, undermining sublimation. In the present world, the value of decency walks head on into vulgarity, especially on television. An instrument of such extreme potentiality to improve humanity's quality of life, with exceptional cases, is misused promoting the erotomanic epidemic. Television disseminates, in every day programming, their version of an erotic paradise in their advertisements.

On May 14, 2004, I was watching a t.v. show in which a woman has abandoned her husband to take another. The reason she gives is that the new one "is good in bed". She takes off her blouse to show her naked breasts. The man then exhibits his penis. This show is a daily presentation. The program is directed by a man called Jose Luis. Whoever dares to assert a preference for morality, as a foundation in human affairs, is deemed a fundamentalist; a sort of fanatic. It is not bad to be immoral, what is bad is to be "moralist". What else but fundamentalists are we human beings?

The epistemic foundation, the fundamentals upon

which one creates every day reality, may be values, or on the contrary,ideologies. The only other alternative to values and ideologies is S- R automaticities, characteristic of animals and of the lumpenized sectors of a society. The lumpen condition is a kind of inhumanity covering the whole planet. The gate keepers of the press and television programming in Puerto Rico, dull the sensibility of the people with vulgarity, and crudeness. Their excuse is that vulgarity and crudeness is what people want. They dump trash on the audiences and then say, "this is what the people want.." On the television media of Puerto Rico there is little space for discussion on good music or literature by leading intellectuals. Many years ago, under the direction of Jack Delano, the government station fulfilled that humanistic mission.

There is an expression attributed to Porfirio Diaz, "Poor Mexico, so near to the United States and so far from God." Malinche, is the Aztec princess, who betrayed her own people. Malinchismo brings into everyday television of Mexico gross imitations of the worse kind of programming from U.S.A. television.

The taste of music follows payola, with the disastrous effect on music of such beauty as the tango in Argentina and boleros in the rest of the Latin America. Traditional Latin American music goes down the drain. On a television interview, Antonio Banderas declared that in his youth in Malaga, Spain, the music of his preference and of his friends was Rock.

His preference for flamenco music came to him in the United States.

A didactogenic sneeze in the USA becomes pneumonia

in the malinchista sector of Latin America. The sneeze of trash television in the United States, becomes pneumonia in the super trash programming on the Spanish television. Cristina, on Univision, gives an hours television space to a group of prostitutes dressed in their professional attire. The style of celebrities is based on enticing the audiences through lubricity.

Don Francisco, the most popular M.C. on Spanish television, held a competition of girls with naked behinds, to find out which one had the biggest and prettiest behind. The winner was crowned, Miss Behind. In another competition the audience selected Miss Sexy. Contestants were asked if they would go to bed the first time they went out on a date. A girl wearing a g-string was asked if she would take it off in front of the cameras, for the sake of the health of a child. Her answer was, 'yes.' What a sacrifice! A program that originates in Mexico discusses AIDS, (Syndrome of Acquired Immune Deficiency). Three hundred thousand Mexicans have this disease. It is calculated that millions will become infected within several years, at the rate of contagion that now exists. Values? Who said values? That is not a push button solution. It is intellectual, and intellect is elitist, the number one sin in this lumpenized learning environment. One advertisement presented a girl in bed, in an erotic pose, "Did you bring it?" she asks, with suggestive overtones. "I forgot," he answers. The light goes out, ending the encounter. The latent message is: Sex is OK if performed with condoms. This is a way of giving legitimacy to promiscuity, and results in an epidemic of unmarried mothers at an age where they themselves should be mothered.

Cardinal Luis Aponte Martinez, in an "Open Letter", June

2,1993, reproached the Puerto Rican Institute of Culture for doing violence to our culture by sponsoring festivals, where the essential values of the culture are violated with rock music, drugs, and styles, copied from the Woodstock festival. Rosario Rangel, in a letter directed to the "Nuevo Dia" July 4, 1993, accused the Puerto Rican Institute of Culture of complicity in the contamination of the plague of vulgarity that was affecting values in our culture. An institution created for the purpose of safeguarding the culture of Puerto Rico reduces culture to the cosmetic domain of aesthetics..

Aesthetics are the expression of beautiful sentiments, but what about the rest of the body of shared understandings of our culture? What about the political culture? Decency is badly bruised by younger generations and by legislators who serve their own pockets, not the people who elected them.

The incomplete definition of culture reaches the minds of our children through the Department of Education. "Words are the instrument of thinking,"said Vigotski. Defective vocabulary is defective thinking. The Institute of Puerto Rican Culture is, in fact, an Institute of Folklore, Art and History. Those have great value. It assumes responsibility for that part of the data bank of culture relative to the expressive authenticity of our artisans, our musicians and our artists. They support exhibitions of art, festivals of artisan work, etc. This is not bad. It is very good. What is not good is to confuse one domain of the cultural construction of reality; the cosmetic aesthetic domain, with the total body of epistemic foundations with which people create their every day life

Television contributes to the cosmetic aesthetics definition of culture with every day programs where trivialities
such as, the private lives of prefabricated celebrities, sexual
scandals, perverse gossip, are transmitted under the rubric
of culture. In the United States, culture, in the aestethic
domain, is used as exotica, as token "evidence" of false
"ethnicities. "Ethnic identities are portrayed on the basis
of trivia such as, "Irish" stew or Saint Patrick's Day and
the color green; Tacos for "Mexicans"; bomba y plena for
Puerto Ricans, etc. (See the author, "Pseudo-Ethnicity is a
Collective Hallucination", in Grito Cultural.)

The pseudo-ethnic assumes an identity based on
cosmetic aesthetic markers. Recently, an executive of the
government television station, at the Festival of San Sebas-
tian, proclaimed a "new tradition. This far fetched "new"
tradition, to be incorporated, was no less than, Rap, the
shabbiest of vulgarities in the name of music.

There was another time in history, when gangs of
thieves over lorded defenseless populations, obliging them
to seek protection behind fortifications and walls of feudal
castles. Now, in San Juan, there are houses which have
become fortresses for protection against an army of occupation in an open city. People in wealthy urbanizations
control entrances to the urbanization with gates. People,
tired of depravation, violence, and confusion, seek security at the price of human rights. Erich Fromm, in *Escape
From Freedom,* traced the rise of authoritarian Fascism in
Germany, to the pattern of repressive tolerance he called
negative freedom. Negative freedom produced a condition

of insecurity in which people were willing to give away their human rights in exchange for security.

These days, in the United States, human rights are violated with the approval of a great sector of the people. We are heirs of centuries of creative thought and positive freedom, attained in some cases by great sacrifices. The fundamental rights conquered, with the heroic sacrifice of lives in previous generations, are often blamed for the prevailing disorder. In search of security people acclaim the 'hard hand'. Hobbes predicted that in the absence of social control, people would pursue their objectives by the most efficient means, which are fraud and violence, resulting in a war of all against all. A repressive punitive model, far from resolving the situation, aggravates it with S-R domestication, based on terror. The medicine turns out to be worse than the illness. The true solution is neither the S- R Patsy seduction nor the repression with an iron hand. Both extremes are inhumane...Patsy's repressive tolerance has nothing to do with self -actualization. Negative tolerance liberates the horses of the Apocalypses. Repressive iron fist style is still worse

Erich Fromm sought the solution in positive freedom and Herbert Marcuse, in non repressive sublimation (*Eros and Civilization*) Positive freedom, with a rational authority, is self actualization in the middle of two extremes, the autocratic iron fist and repressive tolerance. Positive freedom is empowerment of self esteem, and the dignity of human beings.

It is the creative permissiveness that leads to comprehension and supportive relationships among people. Self actualization is transparency, without strangeness, in solidarity, and in the euphoria of community. The return to the ethics condition is the return to authenticity. The process of restoration of the ethics condition is confession in religion, catharsis, with the illumination of logos, in the Freudian theory, and desalienation, for Marx.

The great spiritual teachers of humanity, Lao Tse, Buddha,Socrates, Jesus, Hostos and many others, have attested the condition ethics in which a person loves and contributes to the creation of an everyday reality,. Ethics ennobles existence and promotes self realization. Ethical transparency is communication that flows without strangeness, without obstacles, because it is not impaired by concealment or barriers that create obscurity.

Happiness is pleasure, but there is a great deal of difference between the pleasure that is derived from creativity and love that ennobles the existence, and the pleasure that emanates from the perversities of the polymorph perverse that have no transcendence but a momentary discharge. Authentic love ennobles existence. It is true that all human beings seek happiness, but there is a great difference between pleasure, that becomes distasteful, past the immediate pleasure, and often turns out to be degrading, and the pleasure of authenticity that lasts, creates, contributes, and transcends in excellence. A person rich in self-esteem can be as poor as a church mouse, and still be happy. We quoted in Chapter III: R. Tagore's aphorism, "I dreamed that life was pleasure. I woke up and saw that life is service.

It is true that happiness is enjoyment, but hedonistic pleasure is temporary and does not provide the euphoria of solidarity necessary for existence. When someone asked Freud for a definition of normality his answer was, "A person who loves and works." A somewhat similar answer was given by Marx, when he said, "The alienated person avoids work as if it were the plague." When love and work fail, desublimation brings forth the destructive components of the unconscious mind with the propensities of inconsiderate selfishness, avarice perversions, and Sodom and Gomorrah idolatry of the body.

Transparency becomes blurred at the moment a person commits an unethical act, and, for the sake of face saving, seeks justification. Alienation, from the ethical condition, obscures transparency. In losing the condition of authenticity, he/she assumes the contra-intentional identity, the proverbial, "selling the soul to the devil." The process of encanallamiento begins. There is no word in English to translate this malevolent transformation, that becomes a way of life when comprehension breaks down and people substitute the pristine nature of the ethical condition and become an encanallado.

The encanallado produces a repetition compulsion of infamy with the banal hope of making it true and legitimate with repetition. A puppet repeats the same errors and sets loose the evil purposes of the Caliban encanallado. The encanallado repeats the mendacity compulsively, and persistently, seeking justification in ideology.

The missing transparency imposes the break in conceptual understanding, giving strength to S-R automaticity. He/she who is the cause of bad effects, reduces the power of the ego. The wild horse of the unconscious mind runs loose and fraudulent justifications become a way of life.

Encanallamiento covers the whole planet, in the process globalization, parallel to the globalization of the markets, with brutal incidents of criminality, multimillionaire businesses dedicated to pornography, the sale of arms, drug traffic, and today's terror.. Desublimation opens Pandora's box with rates of insanity never seen before, hatred, necrofilia, violence, addiction, desperation. Emotional problems are multiplied; depression, alcoholism, drug addiction, crime, idolatry of the body, inconsiderateness, selfishness, pervasions. A society immersed in encanallamiento, is geared to the Hobbesian condition.

CHAPTER VI

The Cultural Construction of Racism

I have a dream that one day this nation will rise up to live out the true meaning of its creed ;"We hold these truths that all men are created equal". I have a dream that one day on the Red Hills of Georgia sons of former slaves and the sons of former slave owners will be able to sit down together at the table of brotherhood.

Martin Luther King

A Declaration on race, of the American Anthropological Society, (Sept.1997,) states that "Race" was invented as a social mechanism to justify slavery. Ultimately, race is an ideology about human differences reified and subsequently spread to other areas of the world.

Race, in fact, holds one of the first positions among the ideological fallacies that have caused blood and tears in the historical record of inhumanity. Dr.Ashley-Montagu entitled one of his books, *The Fallacy of Race, The Number One Enemy of Humanity* (New York;World Publishing Co.1964) The ideology of racism has been used for centuries as an epistemic view point to contrive fictions, myths, hallucinations, and fantasies, for concealment of exploitation, and devastation of the dignity of human beings. There are few moments in history when the human mind has been as active in creating justifications for crimes against humanity, as the genocidal conquest of the New World. Few times in history has encanallamiento manufactured justifications for these crimes to humanity to the extent of that moment in history.. The invention of racism, as an ideological cover up of exploitation, became a generalized epistemic foundation, implanting a false consciousness and affirming, as truth, something demonstrably false.

The so called "new world" came to life with a holocaust as infamous as that committed by the Nazis, in our time, against the Jews in Nazi Germany. Victims of terror in the new world were dismembered to induce collective terror. Punishments, such as stripping off pieces of skin with the lashes of a whip, were practiced. A contraption called Cepo was used to place victims in the tropical sun until they died from dehydration. Torturers incinerated victims in bonfires for assumed witchcraft or imagined sins.

The iniquities of that period, to a large extent, have ended, but still, in the middle of the 19th century, Eduardo Galeano tells us, in his classic, *Through the Open Veins of Our Continent,* that there were seventy million peasants, whose fortune consisted of only twenty five cents for a day's work. Galeano calls, 'proxenetas' pimps, those who squander the money plundered from barefoot peasants, while living in their homeland in luxury, ostentation, promiscuity with gigolos for the ladies, and call girls for the gentlemen. Out of the misery of undernourished peasants, they deposit five billion dollars in private accounts in

Switzerland and in the United State banks. There is also the genocide perpetrated on the plantations of the Inirida and the Vaupes, immortalized in the novel, *La Voragine,* by the Colombian author, Jose Eustaquio Rivera. Ciro Alegria, in his novel *El Mundo Es Ancho y Ajeno*, (The World is Broad and Alien) denounces the inhumanity practiced against the original owners of those lands. In recent years, the Puerto Rican actor, Raul Julia, dramatized in the movies the life of Chico Mendez, assassinated by predators of the Amazonian woodland, who cut down thousands of acres of forest daily and killed whoever stood in their way.. Chico Mendez died at the hands of those who profit from destroying the lungs of the planet.

Racism is indeed a set of attitudes and beliefs developed by Western European powers, since the 16th century, stamped in the ideology of their culture. In an article published in the, "Revista Grito Cultural," (number 1 year 1998,) Hector Bermudez Zenon, provides a historical perspective on centuries of oppression against the people of African descent in Puerto Rico. In 1679 the Catholic church excluded those who were not of "pure blood", entrance to the seminary. Still, in 1832 Bishop Pedro Gutierrez de Coz proclaimed that young students in the seminary must be "natives of the island, be of Spanish origin and clean of any bad racial background." In 1849, Governor Prim published an "Edict Against the African Race" that imposed death to free Negroes and slaves who assaulted a white person. It prohibited a master of slaves to exceed twenty lashes as punishment, but the administrators were eager to flatter their owners thus they often exceeded the number of lashes, to the point of causing death to the slave.

Not so long ago, in Puerto Rico, non white musicians had to enter hotels, where they played their music, through the back door. Social clubs, as well as university fraternities, denied entrance to any one who did not pass to the fourth generation test of being white. Ricardo Alegria, who founded the first non racist fraternity at the University, says that the reason given for discrimination in other fraternities was that they, the members, did not want their sisters to dance with a non white. There was a case of a Hotel refusing admission to a Black client. The case went to court. The hotel was found guilty and sentenced to indemnify the offended party.

There is an Institute of Puerto Rican Culture that might as well be named Institute of Racist Ideology. It represents our national culture as a cosmetic assemble of aesthetic trivialities supposed to represent an stereotyped version of three races. The slaves brought to Puerto Rico came from many different places in Africa.. Africa is not one culture as Europe is not one culture. There are many different cultures in Africa. As for the white population of Puerto Rico, it includes the original Spanish invaders, but there are others such as, the Fas, the Galib, the Bruckmans, the Wiscovitch and Petrovitch for example, in my home town.. What about the Corsos of Yauco, at present claiming their share in a pseudo ethnic identity pie transculturated by the so called Institute of Culture? What about the French, many of whom escaped Haiti when the Black population obtained independence from France?. I do not think the O'Neils, the Mac Allisters, McDougals, Mc Clintocks, etc. came from Africa nor from Spain. In proclaiming a racist definition of human beings there is a disavowal of culture.

"We the people, "is a miracle produced by the shared epistemic foundations produced by enculturation. In assuming that human identity is a derivative of genetic inheritance, they are promoting of a racist ideology

Race is a valid concept when applied to animals because animals, in effect, inherit their conduct. Their existence is genetically programmed. If someone teaches them a few tricks, using S-R methodology, animals will not be able to transmit the tricks since they lack the means for abstract representation. A culture encompasses the epistemic foundations with which we perceive in the domains of interpersonal communication, social relations, and work. Perception informs action. If the acquired epistemic foundation with which one perceives, knows, and acts, originates in ideology, the product is an outrage to human dignity, like that of racism...

The problem is that the transcultured racist ideology of our Institute of "Culture" permeates the education of our children since it is the official doctrine of the Department of Education.

The invasion of the island by the United States in 1898 gave birth to a curious state of mind in the domain of racism. U.S.A. observers came to the island and in their studies they concluded that Puerto Ricans are blessed with a democratic spirit, free from humanities number one crime, which is racism.. This would have been a great blessing, if true. But, it was not true. In fact, it operated as a smoke screen to cover up ongoing racist practices. This ethnocentric distortion of our reality originated in an epistemic foundation that prevails in the United States and informs the perception of their people.

There are many differences in epistemic foundations or ways of seeing, between the USA and Latin America. The epistemic foundation defining racism in the United Sates, has been described by Dr. Marvin Harris, under the label of hypo descent. He characterizes the paradigm of hypo descent in the following way : "The rule of hypo descent, is an invention which we in the United States have made, in order to keep biological facts from intruding into our collective racist fantasies. With it we have gone so far as to create Alice in Wonderland kinds of Negroes, about whom people say, "He certainly does not look like a Negro." Consider the case of Harry S. Murphy, the young man who recently announced that he, not James Meredith, had been the first Negro ever to be admitted to the University of Mississippi. "(Harris, M., *Patterns of Race in the Americas*, New York. Columbia U, Press 1976)

On the basis of hypo descent, people in the culture of the United States see two categories of race, White and non-White. Puerto Ricans, as well as all other Latin American cultures, see what has been called a rainbow that includes intermediate categories between Black and White, such as Mulatto, Grifo, con Raja, Jabao, and between Indian and White, Cholo, Mestizo, etc..

Commentators from the United States "saw" with ethnocentric optic a Land of Wonders as Earl Parker Hanson, would have it.. In a book, *Puerto Rico, Land of Wonders*, Hanson declared that in the United States, "a drop of Negro blood makes a person a Negro, and in Puerto Rico a drop of White blood makes a person White." The greatest wonder in this case, is the invention of White blood, since all human blood is red, with types A, AB, B. and O. If you need a blood transfusion, the type of blood, not the so call race of the donor is what counts.

At the Status Commission, Sidney Mintz, declared that, "if a Negro (a Puerto Rican) practiced negative prejudice against another Negro, that was not considered racism". In order to explain away the prevailing iniquities and inequalities produced by negative discrimination against non Whites, Mintz invented the portent of social prejudice. If social, like Friday social, there is nothing to worry about. The question remains, 'Is there a racism that is not social i.e. acquired from the ideological construction of reality of a culture?' This evasion from reality, invented by Mintz, serves the purpose of a cloak to conceal racist practices labeled "social prejudice.". The Inter-American University gave Mintz a Doctor Degree Honoris Causa.

Earl Parker Hanson, Joseph Fitzpatrick, and Melvin Tumin attested that Puerto Ricans were free from humanities number one crime. A recently published book, by the Society for Latin American Anthropology, speaks of the dominant middle class of Argentina as "White" (in quotes). (See: Society for Latin American Anthropology, "Migrants and Identities and Latin American Cities, "1997). If the italics surrounding "White," included all Whites, in all places, that would be closer to the truth. Robert P. Stuckert, in an article, "Race Mixtures; The African Ancestry of White Americans", argues that if the criteria of purity were applied with rigor to the White population of the United States, a very high percentage would then be Negro.(in Paul Hammond ed...*Physical Anthropology and Archaeology*, New York, MacMillan, 1965.) Munro Edmonson, of Tulane University, in a court case in which a person who had lived as White all her life was given a passport as Negro, on the basis of the so called 'drop of blood', had her passport as White taken away. This made a more radical statement than that made by Robert P. Stuckert. (see, "Son Negroes Todos los Americanos," en El Mundo, Septiembre 18, 1982.)

Physical anthropologists, studying human genetics, convened at UNESCO,and prepared a Declaration on Race and Racism, in which they stated that there is no such thing as pure race (genotypical or "Aryan"). (See Declaracion Sobre Raza y Racismo, de la UNESCO,1951.) The Declaration on Race of the American Anthropological Society (Sept. 1997, pg.27) tells us that: 'Genetically there are greater differences among individuals within populations than there are differences between them. No human group can be seen as homogeneous or "pure."'

Don Luis Munoz Marin, in his article "The Sad Case of Puerto Rico." (American Mercury, vol. XV1, num.62, Feb.1929, pp.136-142) refers to the colonial mentality in these words; "Although a community can be ruled by a few men willing to rule it in a nice way, some kind of supporting majority was demanded by the democratic yen. So, a majority was found. To be a member of this majority all you had to do was to proclaim yourself an ardent American, in bad English or in no English at all. If you were a member of the majority, you could become a street-cleaner or a health inspector, or you could recommend some poor henchmen for either jobs." What people with power see, even if it is an emperor's garment type of phantasmagoria, commands respect from those predisposed to please the Poderoso Caballero Don Dinero. Opinions, designs, and models of reality, in accord with the interest of the privileged, prevail in the collective learning environment.

The Brazilian anthropologist, Dr. Octavio Ianni, has pointed out that the Brazilian social scientists acquire the categories of racism of the USA since, in fact, the gate keepers of the profession reside in the United States This acquired mentality is far from Brazilian reality, especially on the question race and racism. The fact is well known that Gilberto Freyre acquired fame and professional prestige with only one phrase in his writings, "The Negro is Closer to Heaven in Brazil,"

"Brazilian social scientists," says Dr. Octavio Ianni, are, "saturated with feelings of inferiority, generated by the naive acceptance of a foreign domination (of the mind)."

Just as in Brazil, many Puerto Rican Scholars did in fact accept the foreign domination (of the mind,) Just as in Brazil, many Puerto Rican Scholars did in fact accept the emperor's garment lens for perception of racism. Jose Colombian Rosario, raised his voice against the colonial mentality. He called for a stop on the concealment of racism in Puerto Rico. Racism should be exposed to the rays of the tropical sun, for its possible cleansing.

Dr. Pedro Munoz Amato recently died. Little of his life was acknowledged in the press. The same day that Munoz Amato died, a salsa singer died. The municipality of Mayaguez declared three days of mourning, with flags at half mast, to honor the salsa singer.. The gate keepers, who assign value to the life work of people ignored Pedro Munoz Amato's contributions to this country of ours, in his dedicated service on the Committee of Civil Rights. The Civil Rights Report of that Committee, edited by Dr. Pedro

Munoz Amato, had historical repercussions in the political culture of Puerto Rico. Exposure made on the Civil Rights Report to Governor Muñoz Marin, led to the release of Nationalists imprisoned during a revolt in the early 1950s. A 'black listing' practice of the police was denounced.. Records so obtained, were returned to the black listed subjects and a court case, is in progress for damages caused by black listing in employment opportunities.

The Social Research Center of the University of Puerto Rico, assigned me a study of the political culture of Puerto Rico, as part of the research program directed by Dr. Pedro Muñoz Amato.. My contribution to the program was published in a book, *Civil Rights in the Political Culture of Puerto Rico,* which won a prize. That study revealed that 54% of Puerto Ricans ignored the basic notion of democracy as government by consent of the governed. Ignorance of civil rights is the same as blindfolded delegation of authority at the polls by the governed. An effective democracy must guarantee the flow of information.. Freedom of expression, and freedom of the press, are aimed to produce that free flow of information. True delegation of authority in the electoral process, would not be valid in the absence of a free flow of information. Civil rights guarantees an electoral process, free from abusive force, coercion, bribery, or extortion. Negative discrimination for political ideas, implants fear and stops the flow of information. Civil rights are an instrumental means to facilitate the flow of information. Faulty information means faulty electoral process. Demagogy depends on faulty information, as foreseen many centuries ago by Aristotle, and nullifies democracy.

Democracy is a term with no substance, if civil rights are not part of the collective conscience of the people.

Cesar Andreu expressed doubts in a hearing of the Civil Right Committee, on the actuality of freedom of information in Puerto Rico.. He denounced the monopoly exercised by the press on the information that should nourish the thoughts of the people. He said that there are four levels where censorship operates:

a) The monopoly of the international agencies of news providers

b) the nonexistence of the right to equal time

c) the ideological base of the owners of these enterprises

d) the capricious personalismo of the owners of newspapers.

An examples of a whim of personalismo is the case of a person in disgrace whose photo was erased in a group portrait to be published in a newspaper. Luis Antonio Miranda testified on this censorship at the Committee of Governor Luis Muñoz Marin for the study of Civil Rights.

At the time of my study, the official creed, sustaining that racism did not exist in our culture, still remained in the yellow press of the island. To test that as a hypothesis, we selected a representative sampling of the population and administered a test on perception.. A set of pictures were presented and the interviewed were asked to group them according to racist identity. This test appears in the book, *Los Derechos Civiles en la Cultura Politica Puertorriqueña* (University of Puerto Rico Press 1965). There was consensus on who was White, Mulatto, Black Jabao, etc. We also asked who were the best looking, the most intelligent, the most respectable, etc. The answers, in most cases, showed preference for Whites and a dislike for non Whites.

A conference, held at the University of Puerto Rico, reported by the periodical,"Dialogue," denounced a supposed negative discrimination against returning migrants from the United States. That conclusion is fabricated out of ignorance of the difference between two different patterns of assimilation, the additive, and the subtractive.. In not distinguishing the fundamental difference between additive and subtractive assimilation, an error with important consequences is made. It affects the support that has always existed between both communities, the one at home and the other on the continent.

As for cultural assimilation, there is no choice except those two modes. The term "subtractive assimilation," was coined by Dr. Wallace Lambert, to designate those who acquire the American culture and give up the culture of their forefathers. In acquiring the culture of the United States as their epistemic foundation of perception, they incorporate the notion of not being who they are. Their communication, their styles of interpersonal relations, their human skills, are as American "as apple pie," yet they do not consider themselves, nor are considered by others, what they truly are.

Instead, they receive a sort of sweatshirt that says, "I am Pororican, Italian, Irish, etc.

Lambert uses the term 'additive assimilation' for those immigrants and their descendants who acquire the culture of the USA but retain the culture of their forefathers. For those, the ethnicity attributed to them, on the basis of forefathers, is correct and authentic. The moment the migrant

Puerto Rican arrives at the airport in New York, he is given the first lesson on the paradigm of pseudo ethnicity. Suddenly, as Venus from the Water, appear so called Irish, Polish, Italians, Afro- Americans,Greeks, Czechs, Jews, etc. Soon the migrant Puerto Rican will learn to call the policeman,"La Jara" (O'Hara), the landlord and the "boss" as the "Jew". Soon he will learn the derisive references such as Dago, Guinea, Greaser, for "Italians", Mick for "Irish", Gooks for Asians, Pollack for "Polish" (as in the film, "Street Car Named Desire"), WASP for a mythical racist aristocracy, Moreno for Blacks, Spic for "Latinos" etc., and "White" for what they are not.

At a conference in New York, student activists ordered Whites to leave the room. There were several professors from the University of Puerto Rico who did not know that in the optic of USA culture they were non White. They left the room. That was not what the student activists had in mind, so they asked the professors to return to the conference.

Pseudo ethnicity Is a form of racism that excludes culture as a determinant of humanization. It deems identity as a genetic product. The migrant Puerto Ricans in New York, in their assimilation to the culture of the United States, are exposed to a didactogenic environment in which racism appears in the form of the stereotype of Puerto Rican as non White as well as in the form pseudo ethnicity.

One of our great writers, Pedro Juan Soto, describes the two contrasting forms of assimilation in the culture of the United States, the additive and subtractive assimilation. In his novel, *Ardiente Suelo Fria Estacion,*there are two brothers. One named Jacinto, assimilated in the culture of the United States, in the manner that Lambert called 'additive' or co-cultural. He returns to the island and immediately enters the networks of interpersonal relations as a fish in the water. Soon he is involved in the affairs of his community, as if he has never been away. His brother, Eduardo, was assimilated in the manner that Lambert calls 'subtractive '.

Having lost the dexterities to enter the network of action to create the every day reality in the community he has a sense of total loss. In acquiring the culture of the United States he acquired the idea that he was Puerto Rican and he felt his Puertorricannesss in his heart.. He has come to his beloved island with his heart filled with desire to be near to his people and be of help to them. However, having lost the dexterities of communication and social relations, based on the epistemic foundations of the culture of his fore fathers, in returning to what he has considered his country, he has the same feelings as when in the ghetto he was told by other pseudo ethnics, "Puerto Rican, Why don't you go back where you came from." He returns to the United States in profound desolation. His homeland, that he loved so much, did not accept him according to a mistaken assumption derived from a pattern of perception of the culture of the United States.

The Jacintos (the additively assimilated) have brought to this island a best of human qualities. There are many testimonials that support Lambert's conclusion that the additively assimilated have the best kind of humanity. Elsita Tio, in a newspaper article, writes "Como Caidos del Cielo" (As Fallen from the Sky,) recognizing that the Jacintos have brought to the island the finest of human qualities. The

additively assimilated do not become agents of transcul-
turation or idols of those desiring des-nationalization. The
paradigms of culture branch off in two opposite directions,
on one side there is ideology or false conscience, and on the
other side are the values, clean and transparent, promoting
human equality, and decency, and dignity, for all human
beings. When the epistemic foundations of enculturation
emanate from values, we are, as Carey McWilliams used to
say, 'Brothers Under the Skin.'There are important sectors
of the people in USA for whom racism is no longer a valid
or significant differentiating factor among people. Black
actors are presented as doctors, judges, and the good guy
policeman, or cowboy. No longer are they presented exclu-
sively in a servant's role. Oprah is a national idol, one of the
four richest women in the United States. Former President
Clinton appeared in the newspaper, embracing, as Latin
friends do, the best boxer of all times, Mohammed Ali.
Condoleezza Wright is Secretary of State. There is hardly
any announcement on television that does not include
Black children or Black actors.

The good news is also contagious. The good news open
the pages of the means of communication, always reluc-
tant to publish what we have written about this subject of
racism.. A Puerto Rican Council Against Racism, which
never before saw coverage in the press, is no longer in
obscurity. The magazine, Grito Cultural, Num. 1, 1998,
has published my article ;"A New Racism Threatens the
Continuity of the Puerto Rican People in History, opening
a discussion on pseudo ethnicity. Newspapers in Puerto
Rico, in the past, never mentioned the question of pseudo
ethnicity. The Journal of America Indigena in Mexico

published, of the author, "La Asimilacion Co-Cultural Es Urgencia Existencial Para Las Minorias Hispano Parlantes en Estados Unidos." Co Cultural Assimilation is an Existential urgency for the Hispanic Minority in the United States. We have argued that the concept of co-cultural assimilation might be considered in educational programs for cultural pluralism. In Mexico, Ecuador, Peru, Guatemala, etc. education aimed at additive assimilation might avoid polarization of ethnicities who fight for the survival of their cultural identity.

CHAPTER VII

Epistemic Anarchy
The Path Toward Nonsense

"The reason education is so important is to make
people aware that the highest of all truth is to
be a laborer of ethical actions."

Eugenio Maria de Hostos

Anyone who dares to disagree with the prevailing dogma in an authoritarian regime is exposed to political persecution, if not death.

Professor Jesus Galindez, from the University of Columbia, wrote a book, *La Era de Trujillo*. He was kidnapped in the streets of New York by Trujillo henchmen, placed on an airplane, and flown to the Dominican Republic. There he was tortured and then murdered. The number of victims tortured and killed by the Chilean dictator, Augusto Pinochet, includes artists like Victor Jara, whose hands were severed, so he could never again play guitar, in which he was a virtuoso. The victims of torture and incineration by the Nazi regime has been calculated at six million..

Much has been written about the outrage to human dignity caused by dogmatic authoritarian systems. There is however, an opposite side to authoritarianism. It does not have the brutality and blood thirstiness of dictatorships, but it also produces undesirable human conditions.. We shall call the opposite side of authoritarianism, 'epistemic anarchy'. Of epistemic anarchy little is known or written, except when Erich Fromm discussed negative freedom in his classical book, *Escape From Freedom*. According to Dr. Fromm, that was the breeding ground for the advent of Nazism in Germany.

The Hobbsian chaos produces a desperate search for security. At the individual level, the mechanism of repression is a simple minded automaticity that ignores sublimation. At the collective level, fear brings forth that automaticity, a rebuke to anyone who sees beyond the animal response of repression. A repressive, punitive model, far from resolving the situation, aggravates it with S-R domestication, based on the terror. The medicine turns out to be worse than the illness. The true solution is neither the S-R Patsy seduction, nor the repression with an iron hand. Between the option of dogmatism on one extreme, and permissive irresponsibility on the opposite extreme, there is a middle point, the 'golden mean', which Erich Fromm called, "positive freedom", and Marcuse called, "non repressive sublimation."

Patsy's repressive tolerance has nothing to do with self actualization. Self actualization and authenticity are attainable in what Erich Fromm called, "positive freedom," and Herbert Marcuse (*Eros and Civilization*, Vintage) called non repressive sublimation. With an S-R animal model in mind, there are two 'black and white' extremes, 'heavy hand' repression or epistemic anarchy. Epistemic anarchy arises from irresponsible permissiveness, the simple minded plague of our times.

In Central American countries, El Salvador, Honduras, Nicaragua, people quite often take the law into their own hands. Recently an example of this going to an extreme, was the report of a lynching in a Mexican town, where three policemen were accused of kidnapping children. Their accusers were true delinquents. A crowd gathered and lynched them Lynching innocent people, induced by interested parties, is a common theme in U.S.A. movies. There is indeed, insecurity produced by criminality in the streets. People do not trust the government to provide an adequate protection to the community. Most people lack any notion of civil rights applied by courts of justice. The fact is, that there is no space for more inmates in the correctional institutions.

Epistemic anarchy prescribes a disavowal of any discipline or control. The treasure of knowledge of great discoveries in the history of ideas, is scorned as idealist, or moon intellectuals. Everyone has in his/her private "book," doing 'his thing' This refusal has nothing to do with critical thinking. It is negativism. Epistemic anarchy returns us to the times when Socrates debated against the Sophists, for whom there was nothing that could be called truth. An ad hoc, "hit or miss" improvisation for the discovery of luke warm water, or as some would say, to discover the Mediterranean, or the wheel, prevails. A collective chaos ends up in a jumble of of disconcerted voices, a Babylonian tower, with a thousand languages, in a multitudinal incomprehension that we have called lumpenization.

In the Hispanic world, radical individuation (me da la

gana) produces the syndrome of ingovernability. Simon Bolivar tasted the bitterness produced by this anarchic individualization where caudillos disintegrated Latin America as one nation. His epitaph was, "I am plowed in the sea." Don Miguel de Unamuno writes on this matter,. "While we do not break this crust of intolerance, of laziness, of envy, of Moroccan pride, there will be neither industry, nor agriculture, nor science, nor art, nor anything. (unpublished Letters of Mr. Miguel de Unamuno, Madrid, 1972.) Realismo magico is not the literary style of Gabriel Garcia Marques. It is the style of life of the people he writes about. Ingovernability breeds caudillismo, the hard counter part of chaotic anarchy

People affected by epistemic anarchy repudiate the notion of "control," considering any kind of control as oppressive, ignoring the difference between abusive, exploitative, dehumanizing control, and guidance, necessary for collaboration in the collective construction of reality. Epistemic anarchy impoverishes humanization in that it creates the lumpen world. In the lumpen world, intellect is disdained. Control based on dialogue, with a foundation in values to enhance human dignity and self actualization, as for example in education, health, sanitation, and communality, is undermined in epistemic anarchy.

Epistemic anarchy, in the American Anthropological Association, creates a dispersion of trivial distinctions that do not embody a respectable academic discipline. Respectable academic disciplines, such as ethnology, linguistics, physical anthropology, and archeology are now substituted with haphazard, ad hoc trivia, such as, anthropology of regional colleges, anthropology of homosexuals, anthropology of agriculture, anthropology of nutrition, anthropology for the liberation of women, etc. Those who own the means of dissemination of information in the press, radio, and television, have the means to program the minds of the people, which in the case of epistemic anarchy, means dispersion in the name of pluralism. Marx's aphorism, "The dominant ideas of an epoch are the ideas imposed by a dominant class," should include, "the establishment entrenches itself with the acclaim of people, as in the present moment, in situations of insecurity." That is exactly how Erich Fromm explained the advent of Fascism in Germany, in, *Escape From Freedom.*

During the civil rights revolution, the middle of the last century, the seed of discord was implanted by demagogic agent provocateurs. A multitudinal incomprehension was then presented as pluralism. If no one is listening, what kind of pluralism is that? It is more like a "jueyera", a dispersion of trivialities, an existential absurdity, a labyrinth of solitude.

C. W. Mills in his book, *The Power Elite*, labeled these corrupt networks, 'the clique,' an academic Mafia composed of partners well versed in methods of how to climb the pyramid of power and professional prestige, outside and in neglect of the merit system.

"Gate keepers," in educational institutions, decide who shall be hired or fired or promoted, who shall receive support for investigation with foundation funds, secretarial assistance, opportunities to publish, travel expenses to participate in international conferences, etc. Under normal circumstances, the decisional process is based on the foundation of values, which means merit. Not so, when the ideology of epistemic anarchy prevails, and then the decisional process is in the hands of the kind of bureaucrat known as 'Juan Batata'. 'Batata', (sweet potato) is bribery, using an institution as pork barrel to create a corrupt network. Juan Batata's standard operating procedure is the quid pro quo of handing out positions and promotions as patronage to friends, who in turn would support his position of power.

Mediocrity immediately stands out. Mediocrity breeds mediocrity. Mediocrity brings about patterns of decisional processes in degrading an academic community that should be a haven of dignity and understanding Where mediocrity takes control, a descent down the scale of excellency becomes visible in universities. An incompetent person is hired, while a competent person is deprived of the opportunity to serve the institution. Juan Batata closes the door to anyone who might exceed his own short intellectual vision. The professional, privileged ruling class, called by C.W. Mills,"The Clique," comes into existence, alien to the professional standards of excellence. Professor Mills describes the Academic clique in these words;. "The clique" turns the institution into a pork barrel in which opportunities, such as ready acceptances of articles and books for publication, allocation of research funds, support for honorific positions in professional organizations, memberships to editorial boards of professional journals, and handsome expense accounts to travel to international conferences, are received by the insiders. Those who have the seal of approval in networks of "the clique" accrue power in the manipulation of decision making processes."

C. W, Mills describes the intrigue and maneuvers

employed by the moguls of the Academic Mafia to create reputations. They control the professional magazines so that if an author desires to publish in those magazines, he/she must count on their approval. Agents of the Academic Mafia, assign their books to be reviewed by sympathizers within their circle. Since true scholars have little time for politics, the field is wide open for the Academic Mafia. A teacher who equivocates the humanizing commitment of his profession, does not fulfill his mission to the extent that he /she falls in irresponsible negligence, or in hard had dogmatism, two extremes that miss the ethical humanizing middle point.

Don Eugenio Maria de Hostos spoke and portrayed his conception of the educator as apostle. Hostos said to this effect, "The reason education is so important is to make people aware that the highest of all truth is to be a laborer of ethical actions." Freud had said something similar in defining mental stability as, "love and work." Freud called, ego,, the spirit of enlightenment, that replenishes us with pleasure in those creations that endure, and in ethical action. A maestro serves the people with devotion if their intellectual formation is guided by teachers who follow a strict criterion of academic excellence, dedication to study, to teach, and to investigate. If that were the case, a community of scholars would evolve who would respect one another for their work, and not for their political preferences or membership in academic cliques.

The Bill of Rights, in our Constitution, prohibits discrimination on the basis of social origin, race, religion and political beliefs. It guarantees a person to sustain his/her ideas and opinions as inalienable rights. Laws and regulations exist prohibiting corrupt politicization. There are norms based on the criterion of academic excellence and dedication. Section 5 of the Bill of Rights of our Constitution, states that: "All people have the right to an education that is aimed to the complete development of the personality, and to fortify respect to the rights of man and his fundamental liberties."

It often happens that Latin American countries have, 'written constitutions,' comparable to the most democratic countries of the world, but these exalted words remain words, and hardly ever attain reality in practice. When a true scholar serves as an executive in the decisional process, the entire intellectual climate of the University attains authenticity. There is then room for improvement on the transmission of knowledge, investigative curiosity, comprehension, and respect, for human values.

The use of institutional resources, as bribes that corrupt the purposes of decisional processes, creates ingovernability. Arbitrariness generates a yearning for an authoritarian leader to put order in the prevailing disorder. Juan Batata's planned disorder opens the door to the heavy hand of those who misuse power, to implant, with blood and fire, decisional processes that constitute an abuse of human dignity.

CHAPTER VIII

Epistemic Anarchy in Education

*"I would like my people to laugh and sing. I like my
people to dance in the streets."*

Popular song…Danny Rivera

For years, Paulo Freyre has pointed out that education is impaired by what he called, "banking education." Banking education means rote memorization, with no understanding. It is imprinted like in a computer's memory. The teacher who gives preference to rote memory, instead of providing understanding, and critical thinking, is implanting S-R associative automaticities lacking understanding of epistemic points of departure and thus of true comprehension. The student repeats, like a parrot, an imprinted text, (a bottle, was the term used in my student days.) The bottle is emptied in the exam and forever lost. This model of education, unencumbered by intellectual understanding, nourishes the continental Latin American habit of rhetoricism (flowery discourse with little substance.)

As often happens with good ideas, Freyre's idea was vulgarized and taken for what it is not. An expression of

Freyre's, "nobody teaches anybody," was taken in a literal sense as a mandate against memorization.

Vulgarizers have done likewise with Marx, taking his statement, "Philosophers have interpreted diverse forms of the world, but what proceeds is to transform it." as an anti-intellectual prescription leading to action without reflection. Freudian theory, which we shall discuss ahead, was also vulgarized as pan sexualism.

Epistemic anarchy leaves the door open to anti-intellectualism. In the absence of intellect what remains is ad hoc S-R 'hit or miss' improvisation. Ad hoc S-R hit or miss improvisation is, in essence, what Freyre called 'banking education' i.e. duplication without understanding.

The injunction against memorization ignores the difference between memorization without comprehension and memorization with critical understanding. Inane S-R 'hit or miss' improvisation to discover lukewarm water is a denial of Freyre. Memorization, with critical understanding, is the authentic road of learning. Some sectors of the teaching profession equate the transmission of knowledge with banking education. In some cases, this matter is making virtue out of necessity. If the teacher is ignorant, what is he/she doing in a classroom? A teacher's obligation is to conduct students in that upward ascent to intellectual growth. If by ignorance, or misunderstanding of Freyre's theory, the teacher does not teach, he /she should leave the position to someone who upholds the importance of education.

A Patsy type "educator" becomes popular among students whose approach to reality has been molded in the S-R didactogenesis, so common in a lumpenized society.

As was previously mentioned, Patsy is a script, described by Eric Berne, portraying a person, male or female, who is so "good" as to bring the bottle to the alcoholic. This is a syndrome that appears in the society at large. Patsy receives full support from students interested in having a good time, while obtaining good grades from "Mickey Mouse" courses

In the classroom, Patsy propitiates acting out by negligent, irresponsible permissiveness, conductive to the pattern of Lord of the Flies.. Lord of the Flies is a story of a group of children shipwrecked on an uninhabited island in the Pacific. There is a gradual process of erosion of social control, progressively crossing the threshold into a Hobbesian condition. Hobbes predicted that where social control is absent, a condition called, "state of nature," develops, where people pursue hedonistic objectives by the most efficient means, which are fraud and violence. Violence prevails. In the story, the strong establish their domination over the weak and end up murdering them as a pastime The learning environment reproduces, what in society, in general, constitutes a pattern of negligent and irresponsible permissiveness. I have visited public schools where the Blackboard Jungle pattern makes it impossible for a teacher to educate his students. Lord of the Flies is reproduced in the Black Board jungle classroom, turning education into anarchy, in the name of expontaneity.. Teachers tell us that in correcting unacceptable behavior in the classroom, they risk their jobs, or more so, might be charged in court. If a male teacher corrects a female student, he runs the risk of being accused of sexual harassment.

There was a time when teachers were free to abuse

students under the shibboleth, "the letter with blood enters." This abusive condition was substituted, in a sort of 'jumping from the frying pan into the fire with permissive negligence,. in ignorance of dialogic permissiveness, and the middle point between iron fist 'authoritarianism and irresponsible permissiveness Patsy's irresponsible permissiveness pattern generates indolence, the mother of all vices. In government programs, Patsy gives away handouts—-passing out the fish instead of teaching people how to fish. Handouts produce a sort of professionalization of mendacity.

Patsy defends his / her style by arguing that the knowledge of today will be transcended tomorrow. Of course it will. But how can, in ignorance, a person improve something he /she does not understand? In the absence of knowledge, what could be improved? How could one surpass or exceed, what one does not know?

It is true, as Tennyson said, "Our little systems have their day. They have their day and cease to be." The Heraclitian dictum applies to knowledge, but in the absence of knowledge the possibilities of carrying the ball forward are few.. In the absence of the knowledge acquired by those who preceded us, there would not be the remotest possibility of carrying knowledge forward. How far would Einstein have gone if he had not known the Universe of Ptolemy, of Newton, of the theory of indetermination of Heisenberg, of the postulates of quantum mathematics?

What kind of intellectual work is that which lacks information? René Thom has said that; "Modern science has been possible to the extent in which theoretical progress has preceded experimentation." (in Guy Sorman, *The True*

Thinkers of Our Time, Seix Barral, 1989). Critical thinking exists, to the extent, that factual data is open to falsification. The eternal upward ascent in knowledge never ends. We stand on the shoulders of giants, as Newton said, on the work of the intellectuals who proceeded us, in the great race toward more and better knowledge. Self esteem is the hope for the intellect, as well as for peaceful existence. The mission of the teacher in a learning environment, eroded of values, requires education that goes beyond simple eradication of ignorance and error.

There is a constitutional directive in the Constitution of Puerto Rico prescribing, "a full development of the personality, the respect of human rights and of fundamental liberties."(Section 5, Bill of Rights, of the Constitution of Puerto Rico). This constitutional directive places the goal of education beyond the eradication of error and ignorance, onto the full development of personality. Such an agenda demands an educational reform that goes beyond bureaucratic cosmetology. Prevention and rehabilitation, in a world eroded of values, requires the implementation of a program of facilitation, with the purpose of fortifying emotional competence and values. Such an educational agenda requires an educational reform that goes beyond the cognitive aspect of human formation to include emotional education.

CHAPTER IX

Acting Out

Today, there are effective means to abolish
pain, anguish, desperation, chaos and violence
entrapped in epistemic windows of the unconscious.

T o understand irrationality one must understand 'acting out.' The irrationality of acting out occurs when the perception and action, in the present moment, is contaminated with mental images acquired in experiences of extreme loss, extreme pain, terror, and catastrophic events of the past. Catastrophic experiences, internalized in the self system, contaminate the 'looking glass' with which the configurations of perception are attained. We have called,' epistemic foundation,' these lenses that function as a looking glass...This looking glass edits our perception of reality.. A simple illustration of how epistemic lenses operate at the emotional level, is that of the young man who has lost his loved one. He looks around and sees a dark and unpleasant surrounding. A couple in love, in the same surroundings, see the Garden of Eden.

The associative part of the mind stores those recordings

of experiences that one could not face when they occurred, due to the intensity of the pain, lack of understanding, confusion, disruption or loss. These are set in motion in unexpected situations, fired by associative triggers, thus contaminating the perceptive configurations of the present. They function like a hypnotic order. Eric Berne calls these dramatizations, "games people play". We might call them "acting out," leaving the word 'play', for a state of mind of happiness and self fulfillment. If one's state of mind is contaminated with painful or disastrous residues of cata-strophic experiences, the disposition to play is ruined. A person whose epistemic foundations are contaminated by mis-emotions, such as hatred, destructiveness, apathy, pain, sadness, boredom, fear, and passive aggressiveness, will have a great deal of difficulty experiencing the upper range of high quality emotions in accord with values.

Freud used free association to unwrap the turmoil of catastrophic emotions. Brought to the surface of conscious-ness, and re-experienced with the emotional charge of the moment, it produced a return to a truly authentic state of mind. What is called 'mental illness' is, in most cases, a func-tion of the activation of those catastrophic lenses that have remained stored in the mind and have returned from the past, in the form of 'acting out', twisting the configurations of the perception of present reality. A person captive in a reactivation of catastrophic epistemes, pays attention to a "reality" different from the reality of the present. Wounds that have not healed are opened, and then attitudes, emotions, and sentiments, that belong to the past, distort the perception of present reality. Trapped inside that psychic snare, consciousness is obscured. Automatic reaction shuts out the light, and darkness invades life. Traumatizations, at the early beginning, leave profound emotional wounds that stifle the emotional growth of a person.

Rene Spitz discovered in a study of hospitalized children, that lack of motherly love can produce permanent damage in a depressive condition, which he called, anaclitic depression. In extreme cases, this depression can lead to immediate death. Spitz called this extreme case, 'marasmus'. This data confirms what Otto Fenichel, a distinguished disciple of Freud discovered, that a child unloved by his/her mother dies. If not dying, his/her life would be a long nightmare. In his book, *A General Theory of Love,* Thomas Lewis, et al, wrote, "Prolonged separation can be fatal to a immature nervous system, as the vital rhythm of the heart rate and respiration devolve into chaos. Sudden infant death is increased fourfold in mothers who are depressed, because without emotional shelter infants die. These authors add, that "raising children attentively, thoroughly, and patiently, immunizes the brain against stress, like the Salk potion protects the body from polio. Love is, and always will be, the best insurance against despair, for which street drugs are the obvious antidotes "'Acting out' brings to the present, painful and distressing sensations, attitudes, and pre - dispositions, which, in the form of looking glasses, distort the perception of the present. Epistemic phantoms, brought to the present, in the form of acting out, trigger irrational action, pain, anguish, combativeness, disillusionment, and compulsive obsessive conduct, etc. The mind contains a record of all past events, especially those of profound loss, pain, fear, anger, loathsomeness, shame, or combativeness.. Upon coming in contact with an S-R trigger, these epistemic files are opened, interfering with the way of seeing, as well as compelling action based on erroneous premises. A scenery of the past becomes present. In sleep, unassimilated traumatizations come back to the present in the form of nightmares. Returned traumatizations may become a threat to the life and security of persons in his/her environment, on those occasions when the cauldron of seething excitement of the unconscious erupts with the rough force of an untamed horse.

A veteran of the Vietnam War entered a restaurant in Bogota. He carried a machine gun in his hand. He began shooting, leaving many dead and several wounded. He "was not" in a restaurant in Bogota. He "was" on the battlefront with the given command from his superior officer, to kill, or be killed. People with a great deal of power may put in action catastrophic decisional processes, derived from anachronic epistemes, endangering the life and security of other people. Jim Jones in Guyana, Adolph Hitler, Manson, the veteran of Vietnam, mentioned previously, and many others, take into their aberrant reality those within their reach. Their insanity contaminates the environment, often causing death and destruction.

Literature makes abundant use of these irrational pervasions of the past. The dramatic nature of 'acting out' becomes the theme of episodes of compelling power. Freud used the literature on mythology abundantly to illustrate the dynamics of epistemic files, the coming into the present, the unconscious past.. Almost every body is contaminated, in a partial way, with psycho-syllogisms of an irrational type. In the book, *Psycho Pathology of Every*

Day Life, Freud reports a multitude of every day leaks from the chamber of horrors of the unconscious.

"Spellbound," is a novel, made into a movie, with excellent actors such as Gregory Peck and Ingrid Bergman. A young man arrives at a mental health institution to take over the management position. His colleague, a beautiful psychoanalyst, acted by, no less than, Ingrid Bergman, notices that this young man loses control of himself every time he sees parallel lines.. Apart from many other complications, the colleague psychoanalyst at last discovers the hidden trigger. Any pattern of undulation onsets the unconscious record of the tragic death of his brother, who sliding off the edge of a roof, at their home, while he looked on, incapable of giving his brother a hand to safe his life. The trigger brings back the feeling of impotent guilt that remained in the epistemic record of not been able to stop his brother's fall.. The roof had undulations. The happy ending, after many complications, is to be imagined. An unconscious phantom, when discovered, fades away, restoring energies mistakenly channeled into 'acting out.'

We all, to a certain extent, 'act out' in a moment of loss of control..Where the file of epistemic phantoms contain fear, the person is afraid of his own shadow. If the epistemic looking glass is rage, a person lives in a permanent war with his fellow humans. In boredom, the person sinks in a miasma of colorless and tasteless indifference. He is bored in a world where there is so much to be done and to be seen, and.instead of doing something that ennobles his /her existence, he /she drowns in a swamp of stagnant waters. In extreme cases, 'acting out' is a sort of nightmare, in which a person feels trapped, becoming an alien to oneself and other people.

.   Oedipus has had a great impact in literature. Eric Berne, in the book, *What Do You Say After You Say Hello?* places Oedipus meeting an old man. The script develops when Oedipus asks the old man, "Do you want to fight?" If the older man answers, "yes,"—- that is his man, says Berne. Acting out, for Eric Berne, is conceived as a script.. Any day, he says, on the corner of 49th Street,, appears Red Riding Hood. At the present moment Red Riding Hood appears allied with hunters wearing the hats of judges. A wave of propaganda makes Red Riding Hood a victim of the big bad wolf–boxer, president, actor like Osbaldo Rios. Brilliant careers end in marginality like that of Mike Tyson.

It was Shakespeare who said that life is a theater. An open epistemic file is triggered and a drama is acted out as in a theater.

Acting out a script, alien to present reality, like Pirandellos' *Characters in Search of an "Author",* who seek a "customer" with unpaid accounts. Unpaid accounts are settled with the wrong customer. An innocent bystander is told, "You are going to pay for that, you son of a bitch." Theodor Reik uses the term, "inaudible voices" in reference to the unconscious nuclei that when activated distorts present day reality.

There is a story, told as a trifle, about a man who needed a jack in order to raise his automobile to change a tire. A neighbor was at home and the man thought he would lend him a jack. As he walked to the neighbor's house, he began having doubts that the neighbor might refuse to loan him the jack. The expectation of being refused grew. Upon arriving at the neighbor's house, he says, "You can keep your dirty jack. I do not need it, you miser." The neighbor does not understand.

Crimes, injustices, abuses, are the plague of humanity. At the moment the epistemic phantom springs into action, the person is not the same. At the moment these incubus enter into action, the least that may happen is a drop in affinity. At its worst, we may commit actions to be regretted for a lifetime, and for which a high price must be paid.. There is dramatism in 'acting out' in, Lady Mac Beth, who compulsively washes her hands, unaware that what she "wants" to wash out, in no way will come off with soap and water What she wants to wash out is not dirt on the body but the dirt in the mind. She had been an accomplice in the assassination of her husband. Subconscious incubus come to life and the person loses the sense of where he or she is. Aberrant epistemic foundations produce malfunctions, as simple as a raised blood pressure, failing an exam, being tongue tied in a public speech, and far worse predicaments. Epistemic foundations operate, as we have said before, as lenses to look inside and outside, as well as serving as a blinder to conceal reality.

In my village, a man went through the garbage cans in the streets, gathering old papers and magazines. These were dollars for him. He "lived" like a millionaire. Alienating epistemic scripts may lead a person to see himself as Sarah Bernhardt, or Marilyn Monroe, Theodor Roosevelt (like in Arsenic and Old Lace), Tongolele, or like the "Savior," who kidnapped Elizabeth Smart.

John N. Rosen, in his book, *Direct Analysis*, relates the case of a patient who turned his oedipal incestuous impulses, toward his mother, into the opposite impulse. Denying his masculinity was a way of denying his incestuous impulses. He portrayed himself as an attractive woman —- so attractive that no man would be able to resist "her" attraction. It took a year of transference psycho analysis to extinguish this epistemic phantom. At the end of his treatment, he accepted himself for what he truly was, a man.

The catalogue of so called mental illness is, in truth, the reactivation of anachronic files. These files contain events that operate as epistemic filters. Contact, with something vaguely similar, triggers the existential clock back into the chamber of horrors of the unconscious, and the anachronic glasses transform reality. The unconscious is a reservoir of S-R push buttons with automatic ignitions. S-R do not think. They react automatically. Understanding is not part of the S-R process. The moment a past trauma is activated, the existential stage is contaminated with unhealthy emotions. In neurosis, the contamination is partial. In psychosis, the transference, from the past to the present, takes complete control of the person. Responses to Rorschach ink blots project fantasies, hidden impulses present in the unconscious emotional life of a person. These latencies, with a life of their own, were compared by Karl Jung to what spiritualists call spirits. Those incubus are the prime material of that which Freud, with the optics of the medical profession, called "mental illness."

A person's capacity to duplicate information and to understand, is reduced, partially or totally, when anachronic epistemic psycho-syllogisms become optical filters, with aberrant readings of reality..That is an every day occurrence in a classroom. A student's attention is triggered off by who knows what, and then his mind is sent away to who knows where. The teacher who does not know the meaning of 'acting out,' misinterprets the lack of attention, not as the unleashing of demons in the unconscious of the student, but as disrespect to him /her as a person. Courts of Justice react likewise. Ignorance of the the automatic character of 'acting out' leads teachers and members of the Court of Justice, to make use of the S-R scheme with repressive punishments, or with permissive irresponsibility.. Both S-R negative punishment, as well as the positive S-R negligent permissiveness with impunity, are a compounding of the felony. Positive freedom means responsibility. We have mentioned before, the 'golden mean' between the extremes of irresponsible negligent permissiveness and the hard hand. There is the middle point, a dialogic comprehension that Erich Fromm called, "positive freedom."

Positive freedom means responsibility. Responsibility is commitment to act for the greater benefit of the greater number and the least damage to stop, or repair, what is needed, so as to bring about authenticity, serenity. dignity, and transparency.. The pleasure of authenticity is euphoria of self actualization. It is pleasure that transcends egoism to attain creative collaboration with fellow human beings.

The S-R scheme produces automatons that are moved by reinforcements. Causality, in the S-R frame of reference, is reinforcement from the outside to produce an automatic reaction. An S-R approach to rehabilitation reinforces the desire and behavior attitudes, leaving intact the events of the past that interfere with the 'desired' attitudes and behavior. It ignores the fact that where aberrant nuclei in the epistemic unconscious remains untouched, the possibilities of remission are few..

Pop psychologists often act as Patsy, in counseling a client not to keep 'anything below his belt.' This is good advise, inside the session, but not outside where it becomes encouragement for the chaotic society we have called lumpenization. However, 'acting out' is not catharsis. Catastrophic emotions are not extinguished in acting out because neither the place nor the event is an authentic duplication of the traumatic past. Outside of session, acting out increases the pain, sensations, attitudes, fears, weariness, disgust, pressures, confusion, and hate, in summary, all the emotional components of alienation. Catharsis produces extinction, which is the correct way to rehabilitation. Catharsis is a Greek word, and implies cleanliness of the mind with transparency free of emotional contamination. Only the truth can make us free..To not keep anything 'under the belt 'or to be advised that one must get it 'off his/her chest'and not leave anything hidden, is exactly what must be done in a psychotherapy session. Those with whom we share life space are not psycho therapists. The people who occupy our existential scene, respond fire with fire, a bad disposition with a bad disposition. Emotions revived with the intensity of the pain, anguish, and terror,contained from the original trauma, are extinguished when, in a therapy session, they are accepted and well interpreted. Outside of session, they are bothersome to others and dangerous.

Freud called 'insight' the light that dissipates the obscurity of repressed catastrophic residues in the mind...Logos is the underlying epistemic foundation that Freud called insight. What Freud called intra vision (insight), emerges, with its humanizing emotions and its inherent ethical condition. Logos is that kind of intra illumination that many centuries in the past Greek philosophy conceived as the verb, which Christianity, in turn, conceived as divinity. Anthony Mello uses the term "illumination" for this primordial authenticity. The emotional crisis ends when interpreted correctly and accepted.. The moment we recognize the truth that makes us free, affinity, and creative emotions, are recovered. This is a very dramatic moment. Transparency is regained with its contents of immanent ethics where disintoxication of epistemic phantoms is performed. The recovery of innate, misused,or unused, intellectual and emotional energy, for an effective control of ones destiny, is an adventure with which nothing can compare. Returning from those labyrinths of a warped existence, the moment constitutes a marvelous experience. On the face of the person appears a brightness, the purest expression of authenticity and happiness. The psychic energy, used inadequately in 'acting out', is liberated, restoring attention, perception, and action, regaining the capacity of insertion in the everyday decisional processes, with affinity, understanding with critical rationality, and with consciousness of the future.

The doors are now open to conceptual comprehension and to emotional affinity and creativity. Those are the true conditions for the journey on the river of decisional processes in the company of others. Energy associated with catastrophic emotions is now distilled. Where there was irrationality there will be serenity, compassion, and comprehension. It expands the existential space and frees badly used energies. Where there was weakness and despair, true empowerment appears.

In the past, and in some religions, that liberation was seen as an exorcism of a malignant "incubus." In fact, what happens is that the Freudian therapeutic goal is accomplished, "where the id was, the ego will be". The lack of meaning in 'acting out' coincides with Frankl's noogenic neurosis. This disappears, and new horizons of authenticity make a person more compassionate, more understanding, and more tolerant. The disassociated nucleus contains evil impulses, which are ready to harm oneself and others to vanish, leaving a clear version of serenity.

Sigmund Freud postulated the ego as a rider on an indomitable steed called the id. The ego is in a permanent siege in a sea of darkness formed by antisocial impulses of the Id. The Ego controls those impulses, the same way a rider does on a wild horse. The id is a abyss of incestuous impulses, of corruption, depravation, perversion, and all kinds of antisocial impulses. Karl Jung called the hidden part of the personality, "shadows" that he characterized as the recipient of all" uncivilized desires and emotions that are incompatible with social standards, of which we are ashamed." Psychoanalysis is a special kind of education to recover logos with innate value commitment and rationality for self actualization. The epistemic foundations in which thought and emotions are founded are as important in psychoanalysis as in education. Psychoanalysis and psychotherapies have developed effective intervention strategies for the attainment of mental health. However,.the high cost of this professional service exceeds the income possibilities of the less privileged members of a society.

Only the opulent sector of society have access to mental health services. Today, there are low cost effective means to achieve intellectual transparency and emotional intelligence, the awareness of epistemic foundations in the mind that produce the way of thinking, and with that, the way of acting. We shall discuss them in the following chapters.

Hidden or repressed emotional aberrations, recorded in the mind, are brought into consciousness by means other than traditional logic.

Actually, logic or intellectualization operate as defenses to avoid confrontation of repressed unconscious experiences. Victor Frankl quotes B de Spinoza, "Emotions that cause suffering stop as soon as a clear image of it is formed". (Affectus qui passio est, desinit esse passio simulat que eius claram et distinctam formamus ideam.) A clear image is not a report lacking emotions. An authentic clear image opens the doors of comprehension, and then that which before was confusion becomes understanding. Transparent intelligence, ethical awareness, and a high emotional tone called happiness, are outcomes of the returning from those labyrinths of trapped energy, stored in the unconscious.

The brutality of a war costs lives, pain, tears, and desolation. History is a permanent record of destructive irrationality in so many instances misguided by dehumanizing ideologies. How much blood has been spilled on the battlefields in never ending wars? ;Moors against Christians, Protestants against Catholics, slave hunters against their innocent victims, defenders of the "true" Faith against infidels, idolaters, oppressors against oppressed. How much hate in xenophobia, in envy, has been eternally corrosive of affinity and friendships? How much "cainism" began with the biblical Cain, throughout history? How much cruelty and dehumanization in genocide? Ignominious acts, such as the holocaust in Nazi Germany against the Jewish people, still shudders the conscience of humanity. There are many instances in which the dehumanizing Golem makes its presence, as with the holocaust of the Turks against the Armenians, of the Khmer Rouge against the Cambodians, and, in these days, the slaughter between the Africans in Rwanda, and Burundi of Hutus against Batusis (three millions dead), and the Janjaweed massacres performed as so called "ethnic cleansing" against Blacks in East Africa.. The extermination of the original inhabitants of our America is repeated over and over in historical process of encanallamiento. It is a history stained with blood. Evil purposes in the didactogenesis of our modern history are present in so many ways.

Put a pair of roosters in front of one another in a bloody fight to end in death of one of the contestants. If you are a fanatic of cock fights, it may never occur to you how it is possible that one can enjoy seeing two animals killing each other in such a bloody, brutal, and cruel way. Put a pair of horses, or ferocious dogs, or a bull, in front of a torero, a gladiator in front of a lion, or two modern boxers in front of a roaring audience shrieking, "kill him." Even the two candidates for the presidency of the United States, agreed with each other, in a television debate, that they would pursue the terrorists and kill them. For the Chilean people, whose democratically elected president, Allende, was murdered with the aid of the CIA, and then substituted with one of humanities bloodiest assassins, a terrorist, is not clear.

In recent years, an investigator at Yale University designed an experiment to measure the extent to which "normal" people were able to act like the torturers from the Nazi German concentration camps. A group of students were assigned the position of "trainers "of a group of "learners." The participants were told that the purpose of the experiment was to find out to what degree punishment affects memory. A group acting the part of "trainees" were kept separated in different rooms. When making a mistake, the trainers would punish the trainees with an electric shock. The "trainer" assumed that the shock was indeed received by the "apprentice" in the other room. They could hear the shrieks of pain, the wailing screams, and howls of agony and despair. The subjects, of course, did not receive any punishment, The proclaimed intensity of the electric shock was increased following each error. "Trainers" were given information as to at what level the electric shock could be fatal.. The experiment progressed and the screams increased. Trainers increased the punishment with every mistake, upping the voltage as high as 450 volts, sufficient to kill anyone. The signs of terror were simulated, but the trainers did not know that. Milgram concluded that the propensity to become a torturer was in every one, if allowed. Give a man or woman, in these days, a rifle or a ton of mortal bombs. Give him/her immunity and point out where the enemy is. Order him or her to destroy this enemy. He/she will obey the order.

Who does not know about the pilots who empty their lethal loads on defenseless people, in a mass murder of women, children, homes, and all that life has given them. Who does not remember Lieutenant Calley who massacred hundreds of defenseless old men, women, and children, in a village in Vietnam. "Normal" people indeed were able to act like the torturers of the Nazi German concentration camps.

A colleague of mine, from the University of Puerto Rico, Professor Jose Enrique Lausell, told me about a visit he made to one of the ships that took part in the Gulf War. The captain inflated his chest with pride, when he related to the audience of tourists, that his tomahawk rockets, from 1000 meter range, fired on the city of Baghdad. Jack the Ripper, compared to this man, was a little lamb. Those same rockets were able to carry atomic heads, 100 times more destructive than the bombs dropped against the civilian population of Hiroshima.

I remember sitting next to a soldier from the Vietnam War, while flying from New York to Los Angeles. I asked him how he felt when he killed a human being. He answered, "Have you ever gone deer hunting?" I replied negatively. He then continued, as unpreoccupied as if we were discussing the weather, "You feel bad with the first one you kill, then it's routine."

No need to ask why movies of sex and violence have captured television space in our homes. The id is a source of powerful energy. If kept under control, "the untamed horse" moves mountains, creates civilizations, and controls diseases. Sigmund Freud said in, *Civilization and its Discontents*, "There, where the inhibitory influence of civilization fails, man is a savage beast, alien to any consideration that serves in order to protect the life of fellow human beings".

Where social controls are suspended, the demoniacal strengths of the id, with its perversions and antisocial tendencies, come to the surface. If a person commits an act, without ethics, he /she unauthorizes the ego while activating the cauldron of the devil that vomits fire like a volcano. The power of the mind is then put to the purpose of giving legitimization to the unjustifiable act.. That is the breeding grounds of ideology.. There is a compulsion to repeat unethical acts, that we have called encanallamiento. Among the unethical ideologies, in the modern world, there is the prevailing definition of aberration as a nervous problem. Governments prefer to define the cause of emotional problems, as "nerves", to be treated by medical doctors. The drugs prescribed by psychiatrists are addictive with results far from self actualization. Pills dispensed by medical doctors, specializing in psychiatry, are not expensive, and if it is a nervous problem, the state is absolved from any responsibility for the didactogenic functions of the environment.

The terminology best known to Freud came from his profession, medicine. He called symptoms, "the diverse configurations of 'acting out.'" This terminology led to an organic conception of acting out. However, Freud rejected the organicistic view of the mind, He wrote that, "The intellectual training of medical doctors does not enable them to understand superior intellectual processes except as a function of anatomy and physiology "(*The Question of Lay Analysis*, New York, 1953.) In so doing, he disqualified medical doctors, qua medical doctors, to perform psycho analysis with an organicistic view point. One might conclude, therefore, that the assignment of competence to medical doctors, without additional preparation in psychoanalysis, to deal with 'acting out,' is a form of irrational 'acting out' on the part of the government.

CHAPTER X

Emotional Education

*If you want to be an engineer, a medical
        doctor, a lawyer,an architect, you must
study these subjects. But few, if any feel
the need to study the most important subject,
to be a human being.*

Erich Fromm

In the Third World, hundreds of thousands of human beings die premature avoidable deaths. Life expectancy is half that of the developed world.. Unhealthy life conditions, such as, lack of medical assistance, contaminated water, malnutrition, illnesses easily controlled in the world of high productivity, and diseases that no longer affect the lives of people in the world of high productivity, such as parasites, tuberculosis, uncinariasis, malaria, etc., are endemic in the Third World.

The material poverty in the Third World is immense. A good number of the populations earn less than a dollar a day. Eighty percent of the world's population live in the Third World, with 828 million children suffering from hunger at this very moment. 45,000 of these children die every day.

President Lula Da Silva of Brazil has said that poverty is a weapon of mass destruction. The children abandoned in the streets of Bogota, or any other metropolis of the Third World, clamor for a piece of bread to lessen their hunger, or sniff glue which destroys their lungs. Perverts pick them up on the streets to sodomize them. Some are sold for prostitution and child pornography. Kidnapped children in the streets of the Third World are a plague. In Guatemala alone, 400 children have been kidnapped this year.. A Latin American Information Center has been created to account for the increasing rates of children disappearing everyday. The tragedy of families, who survive as scavengers in the garbage dumps of big cities, is a shame for the opulent waste makers of the planet. Poverty generates illiteracy of the letters and of the emotions. Meanwhile, the privileged countries waste 800 million dollars in armaments to equip the occupation army of their own country. These days, the United States spends 225 billion dollars in a war in which cities, that are a monument of humanity, are destroyed A total of 425 persons on this planet have more money than half the population of the earth. Seven families own 89 % of the wealth of El Salvador.

A mogul of Capitalism in Colombia, one of the poorest countries of the world, is described in these words, "Julio Mario Santo Domingo owns Avianca, Sam and Aces, television and radio Caracol, the newspaper, El Espectador, and Cromos magazine, Celular telephone industry, (Celumovil), the Distribution of Renault, Bavaria and Aguila beer, Santander Bank, food processing industries, exports of shrimp, glass manufacturing, Colombian insurance, (Colseguros), and even the water the Colombians drink. All this is controlled by this man." (see, Gerardo Reyes, *Biography of Don Julio Mario*, ediciones B 2004)

Humiliation, pain, tears, death, and terror, are the existential setting of the poor in the planet. In his book, *The Right to Be Intelligent*, Venezuelan educator, Luis Alberto Machado says that, "The first need of the underdeveloped countries is productive efficiency. Sustainable development is not possible as long as intelligence is wealth for the privileged. Neither is it possible to have peace on the earth. To work for intelligence is to work for peace." Productive efficiency is not possible "while the wealth of intelligence is not evenly shared," says Dr. Machado.

Dr. Machado, conceives intelligence as the most violated human right in the world we live in. As a result of that violation, a good portion of humanity is deprived of the opportunity for a full development of innate creative and intellectual potentialities. This lack of educational opportunities, is more than a violation of human rights: it is mutilation: physical and emotional.

Extreme poverty creates what Fanon called, "The Wretched of the Earth." In search of employment opportunities the Wretched of the Earth drown in the water of the Mona channel trying to reach the shores of Puerto Rico, or perish from dehydration trying to cross the border between Mexico and the United States.

With a philanthropic point of view, some governments provide food stamps, educational affirmative action, health and nutritional programs for the poor.. All that is very good. Few people would say, like Luis Alberto Machado, in his book, *The Right to be Intelligent.*, "Give them back the most violated of all human rights, 'The Right to be Intelligent.' William Purke maintains the thesis that, "Cognitive learning increases when self concept increases. "(William W. Purke, *Self Concept and School Achievement,*N J. Englewood Cliff 1970.) Low self esteem reduces that which Erik Erickson called, "basic trust," including a low level of acceptance that interferes with the acceptance of information.

The restoration of self esteem, and the level of acceptance combining cognitive education with emotional education, is our concern in this book. Much has been written about illiteracy of the letters and about methods of alphabetization. Of emotional illiteracy, little is known. except for the sociologist psychoanalyst, Dr. Erich Fromm in, *Escape From Freedom,* where he has stated the question of emotional education in the following words," "If you want to be an engineer, a medical doctor, a lawyer, an architect, you must study these subjects. But few, if any, feel the need to study the most important subject, to be a human being".

Emotional illiteracy interferes with the proper use of intelligence as well as with a proper self concept and self esteem. The incidence of school desertions in the world of the poor, even in the rich countries, is enormous. Transmitting knowledge to a student "absent" for lack of attention is the same as "tilling the sea," to use Bolivar's reference to the ungovernability of the people of Latin America. Without attention, there can be neither communication nor correct reading of the information transmitted by the teacher.

Emotional impoverishment includes the rich people that Andre Gunder Frank calls the lumpenbourgoisie. Emotional illiteracy kills many people on the streets of our planet. It sows the streets with terror,and death, crippling human lives in accidents on the highways, addictions, and delinquency. In the lumpen sector, repressed emotions surface at the slightest provocation, even a fleeting glance may trigger a violent reaction.

Wickedness multiplies in the style of the Gresham law, in the process of encanallamiento that generates a repetition compulsion of anti social acts.

In an emotional illiterate society, there are cults, diviners, astrologists, and sexologists, to promote erotomanic concerns, as well as the hidden persuaders, denounced by Vance Packard, stamping in the minds of people the false notion that an impoverished level of acceptance can be replenished with consumerism. Insecurity prevails in the streets. Delinquency becomes more virulent everyday in places like Mexico, El Salvador, Nicaragua, Honduras, Guatemala, Colombia, Peru, and Argentina..

The bad currency, in human relations, substitutes the good currency.

Emotional illiteracy, in a country like Colombia, produces a civil war, with four Presidential candidates and a Minister of Justice assassinated.

Hundreds of judges have been corrupted with money from narcotic traffic.

Bombs explode in public places, in government offices, and on airplanes, producing a nightmare of terror. It has caused many Colombians to abandon their homeland, at any price. (El Hueco, Castro Caycedo,1989).

The primary cause of death in Medellin is from interpersonal violence. That which is reality in Colombia, is an equally terrifying reality in El Salvador, Nicaragua, Mexico,

Guatemala, Peru. Many of our compatriots in Puerto Rico escape to Orlando, Florida, in search of tranquillity which their homeland is not able to give them..

Many teachers, influenced by the general trend of permissiveness, assume a Patsy type of "facilitation." Permissiveness, gives rise, in extreme cases, to the pattern we have called, Lord of the Flies. Lord of the Flies, in a Blackboard Jungle, are beyond reach of the educational process. Nowadays, the teacher in the classroom is faced with a considerable number of students absent due to inattention. These students cannot duplicate, retain, or understand, the information received from the teacher.. If any learning is to take place, in these circumstances, it would have to be of the type that Paulo Freyre calls "banking," (i.e.memorization without understanding, extinguished the day after the exam.) Without communication, the possibilities of a correct reading of the information transmitted by the teacher is minimal.. Students are lost in a tangle of unconscious reactions, emotions, sensations, feelings, attitudes, and irrational predispositions, produced by S-R reactivations.

Lord of the Flies, in a Blackboard Jungle, commit atrocities against teachers in schools. In a school in Colorado there was a massacre, a similar attack happened recently in Eugenio Maria de Hostos's school, in Trujillo Alto. In the town of Comerio, a student stabbed a teacher to death because, "He did not like him." or whosoever the teacher stood for. I have visited schools where a teacher can not do his/her duty with dignity. When self esteem is low, the level of acceptance is low. Comprehension and intellectual achievement is at a minimal level.

The Office of Youth Affairs of our government in a recent study of a sample of 4,591 respondents, between the ages of 13 and 29 years of age, found that only 3% of these young people has ever read a book. Their main interest is in "looks, (appearance)" and in consumer goods. Everyday the reading sector of the population decreases in a constant descent into functional illiteracy.

Government funding of education has brought forth a bad currency in educational institutions, that Professor Ismael Rodriguez Bou, called "chinchales." Authorized as a University, by the Higher Education Council, a low quality institution operates as a lucrative business. Tuition money is the first consideration on their agenda. Chinchales promote negligent, permissive, and acriterial teaching, since their priority is tuition Since tuition money is the number one priority, 'Mickey Mouse' courses, in these Mickey Mouse Universities, prosper and flourish with the acceptance of unqualified students.. If knowledge is conceived as unnecessary, education becomes, what my students at the University of the City of New York called, 'rap', or 'Mickey Mouse' courses. The good students avoided those courses. Rap today is a style of spoken hassle (bochinche)," chanted profanities accompanied with drums.

The notion of intellect as elitist is held, of all places, in many universities, by sundry professors and their students who misread Paulo Freyre's theory (see chapter 8). Students in Mickey Mouse courses receive good grades in return for their approval of the teacher. Professor Juan Duchesne, in "Revista Fundamentos("num 3-4 1996), writes on this subject. "The door keepers of the university reward under achievement and penalize the good student in his search for understanding of deep and complex problems. For unproductive students, and in some cases antisocial students, there are allowances so as to retain them. "Students are admitted and retained as long as the University receives federal allowances for them. The academic standards 'go down the drain' in order to keep unsuitable students whose tuition is the first priority for the chinchal type of institution. Mickey Mouse education accomplishes the aim of maintaining these unsuitable students. Professor Antonio Fernos, from the Inter American University, writes "there are thousands of graduates very badly educated. We have, in effect gone back to a world where talent is despised, and coarse things are preferred: gross, shrill, and degenerate." Poorly informed students depend on sagacity to manipulate the system rather than a competent performance. Professor Carlos J. Ramos, commented in an article on the commercialization of education, "If a teacher does not pass a determined number of students, he incurs the suspicion of not being able to teach."

Rejection of a candidate, who is applying for an academic position, for the "reason" of been "overqualified" has been a common practice under the rule of mediocrity. There is a case of a University that announced in the media, that 'they' (teach) the most. Teach," (enseñar) also means to show. The announcement was made by a sex worker in brief clothing, promising to (enseñar) show more. There are also a considerable number of teachers who misconceive facilitation as downgraded education.

In Chapter V, we mentioned Eric Berne's diagnostic category of "Patsy". Patsy's script, in the theory of Eric Berne, is the personification of permissive irresponsibility that produces the effect of "repressive tolerance," a reaction formation against unconscious repressive propensities. Reaction formation is a very low level kind of transformation of the unconscious.

CHAPTER XI

Education to Abolish Emotional Illiteracy

*The advanced industrial society has all the means
to attain a society without war, without oppression,
without poverty, and without waste.*

Herbert Marcuse

*"The main objective of the university should be the
creation of men free in their spirits, men who do not
yield the creative potentialities of their souls to nothing
in this world."*

Jaime Benitez

The home, according to Fromm, is "the psychic agency of society".

The quality of parental love, intimacy, and positive emotions in home life is failing, while communal values are corrupted with drug dealers, thieves, and indecency, in the means of communication. Sex and violence, as the means of communication, contaminate the didactogenic environment, modeling an erotomanic epidemic with 49% of births from preadolescent mothers.

Many homes are lacking in love. Homes, communities, and schools, are didactogenic environments that are failing in their humanizing function.

Emotional illiteracy is epidemic in the modern world. Sublimation fails, and desublimation brings forth the horsemen of the Apocalypses, with the evil propensities with brutal incidents of criminality, pornography, the sale of weapons and drug trafficking. These become multimillion-aire business enterprises, with the prospect of corrupting government agencies, judges, policemen, etc. Emotional illiteracy is leading the world to the worst kind of human impoverishment. Murders, accidents on the highways, addictions, that generate delinquency and sow the streets with terror, increasing the incapacitation of hundreds of young people, are a daily occurrence. Emotional distur-bances are legion in our time. One out of every four persons in Puerto Rico needs emotional education. Remedies must be sought for effective prevention.

Where sublimation fails, it leaves us exposed to the destructive components of the unconscious. Human poten-tialities are wasted in street violence. Governments, as we have said in Chapter VIII, prefer to see emotional problems as a matter of 'nerves'. "Pills dispensed by medical doctors, who have specialized in psychiatry, are not expensive and if it is a nervous problem, the state has no responsibility for the didactogenic effect of the learning environment. Drugs prescribed by psychiatrists are addictive, with results far from self actualization.

Against the possibility to abolish emotional illiteracy that blocks intelligence, as well as the innate ethical condi-tion, there are institutionalized barriers which are difficult to circumvent. M. Scott Peck says, "I've often thought that there would be savings if we could develop some program of mental health education in our public schools, but I know we wouldn't get away with it. People would object to it. There is an anti mental health movement in this country (U.S.A.)." (M. Scott Peck, M.D., *The Road Less Traveled*, Pg. 143)

Government agencies in Puerto Rico, are convinced that more policemen, more and better armaments for the police, more effective means of repression, more cameras to watch public places, etc. are the solution to the aberrant behavior that results in a civil war, declared in our streets, where so many young people, still in the flower of life. are being killed. In fact, the 'hard hand' policy generates more inmates in prison, and when there is no space they are released. The term, "correctional" to describe jails, is an euphemism. They are, in fact, schools of high crime.

Graduates come out with a degree in criminal organization. Impunity ends up in re incidence, multiplying the problem. Correctional institutions proliferate, where schools with emotional education programs should be.

Each inmate in our overcrowded prisons costs $76 dollars a day, for a total of $3.43 million dollars a year. Police, and the system of justice, costs as much. By comparison, a University student costs the state about $7.00 a day. Enormous resources are employed in police protection, electronic surveillance, and jails, but the accompanying human insecurity and stress remain.

The S-R scheme, applied by courts of justice, and elsewhere, does more damage than good, as our poet, Edwin Reyes has quipped, "la mano dura no cura" (hard hand does more damage than good.) Neither does irresponsible permissiveness.

A world created in the S-R model, neither the repressive punitive hard hand, nor the irresponsible permissiveness, engender emotional illiteracy. Both miss the middle point of positive freedom, as exposed by Fromm, or repressive sublimation, as proposed by Marcuse. Self esteem is the hope for a peaceful existence. The person who at an early age was submitted to experiences of abandonment, or any other modality of negligence or violence, will have a great deal of difficulty in feeling kindness, beauty, or any other value. His or her emotional intelligence has been injured.

There is an urgent need to advance humanization by means of emotional education. The development of thinking, at its optimum potentialities, is today a possibility. We are proposing a low cost educational program, combining academic excellence and reciprocal co-counseling, under competent supervision, to extinguish experiences that trap units of awareness, and interfere with the transparency of intelligence. An enhanced self concept increases the level of acceptance, and with it enlightenment, and authenticity. This low cost effective technique should rehabilitate and return the person to causative responsibility. People living in under developed countries need low cost education, without sacrificing excellence, to assist students in their eternal ascent to knowledge and the abolition of emotional illiteracy.

The prevention and rehabilitation, in a world eroded of values, requires the implementation of an educational program that combines learning with emotional facilitation. The model of education used in developed countries is costly and completely out of reach for the people of the Third World. Aside from the cost, there is not much to be gained in copying a model whose merits are questionable.

Puerto Rico invests over half of its national budget to maintain the educational bureaucracy. On March 14, 2001, a local newspaper gave the grade of "F," to the Department of Education, due to the huge incidence of illiteracy. It is difficult to understand why 53% of the population suffer a certain degree of illiteracy, (quoted from Carmen Dolores Hernandez, in her article, "Illustrious Illiterate" in El Nuevo Dia, July 27, 2000, pg. 141.) She also quoted that there is a drop- out rate of 55% each year. Of the 55%, a considerable number of these students enter the ranks of delinquency, according to criminologist, Pedro Vales. The educational deficit reflects that 87% of the students who graduate from Secondary school, arrive at the university with deficiencies in the basic dexterities of language and mathematics. Without these basic dexterities, the possibilities for success are scarce. Full development of personality, in my opinion, can only be attained by emotional enlightenment that increases self-esteem. High self esteem increases the level of acceptance, which in turn increases the eagerness to learn.

Our government intends to meet the problem of criminality, through education in values in the schools. To say anything against such a proposal is like affronting Mother's Day. if the emotional illiteracy remains, education in values may result in a waste of time.

Ask a convict why he is in prison, and prepare yourself for dissertation in values, as good as the best. Ask the ex Secretary of Education, Victor Fajardo, now in jail in

Puerto Rico, why he stole millions of dollars from school students, money that had been assigned from the national budget. Ask Dr. Yamil Curie why he stole millions of dollars assigned to Aid programs, or ask the clergyman accused of misbehavior, why,? and you will realize that they did not commit these crimes because of lack of knowledge of values.

Anti social attitudes and intentions inhabit the subconscious part of the mind and manifest themselves in 'acting out. Catastrophic emotions, in re-stimulation, transform a person into an agent of destruction. Emotional illiteracy impoverishes the human condition. To attain an ethical condition, emotional illiteracy must be abolished, in order to open the gates to human values, such as decency, honesty, compassion, and respect of human rights, leading to creative self actualization.

Full development of personality can be attained by emotional enlightenment in the school curriculum. Where alienation prevails, that part of the self, we shall call, 'counter intention', takes over, in destructiveness of self and others. Counter intention is the activation of catastrophic images of pain, sadness, terror, and loss, that become epistemic windows, reducing self esteem and activating catastrophic emotions, sensations, feelings. and attitudes, thus irrational predispositions. The recovery of innate, misused, or unused intellectual and emotional energy, for effective control of ones destiny, is an adventure with nothing to compare... Creative and generous propensities, immanent to human beings, must be brought into the open, eliminating the prospect of Mr. Hyde, that besieges us all. Freedom from the chains of counter intentional blocks against authenticity, gives life to the authentic self. Transparency, attained by emotional education, is the way to that enlightenment and happiness.

Emotional enlightenment takes place when the student has learned to see below the surface, to discover the epistemic root of thinking and action. The awareness of the premises, in which thoughts and emotions are founded, is of fundamental importance in psychoanalysis, as much as in education. Psychoanalysis is a special kind of education that promotes rationality, transparent intelligence, and ethical awareness. Creative enthusiasm, serenity, and that high level of emotional intelligence, called happiness, must be brought to life by extinguishing catastrophic emotions that transform a person into an agent of evil. Education, according to our constitutional directive, goes beyond eradication of error and ignorance to emotional enlightenment. Emotional education should compensate the deficit in the learning environment of the home and the community, in a society in crisis.

The school remains as the last hope to face the problem of emotional illiteracy. The educational system must take the rudder of a sinking ship in a lumpenized society, in order to free a student of the barriers that impede his/ her ascent to knowledge. Teacher education should follow the educational model established for students of psychoanalysis. This should consist of a didactic process to acquire the necessary sensitivity to deal with emotional problems. A teacher, worth that noble name, should know that he /she is not a simple transmitter of information. If it were a matter of only transmitting information and nothing else, nowadays, there are electronic devices that can do that. A teacher must understand that his/her job as a teacher is an ennobling mission.

Maestro, (master) illuminates the obscurities of ignorance and error, step by step, finding a way out of the tunnel of irrationality, injustice, error, and ignorance. Maestro implies, as always, a great responsibility for those whom they lead as disciples. Of the ennobling mission of the teacher, spoke our Eugenio Maria de Hostos. One of our most distinguished writers, Abelardo Diaz Alfaro, personified the model of authenticity for teachers, in the character of Tello Merced, a teacher who stood at the height of human dignity in a jibaro community, and deserved the honorary name of maestro. A teacher who ignores that humanizing commitment becomes a "Mister Rosas", portrayed by Abelardo, in the story, "Santa Clo Arrived at the Mountain School." Teachers should be retrained in the understanding of epistemic foundation, for it is the base from which knowledge stems.

True knowledge means awareness of the premises that serve as foundation of thought configurations with alternative entrances into reality. Although knowledge is not a strait jacket, its flexibility should not be confused with the dispersion we have called 'epistemic anarchy.' Intellectually responsible dialogue promotes the flow of information, illuminating obscurities of ignorance and error and perhaps, of ill intentions   An educational reform is needed, but not for cosmetic changes in beaurocracy, but with a commitment to return the true meaning on enlightenment. The present moment requires an educational reform, placing the abolition of emotional illiteracy as an objective parallel to the ascent in knowledge. The creation of a human being, capable of putting a stop to violence, rapacity, wars, the destruction of the forests, the contamination of the environment, the deterioration of the layer of ozone, of the air that breathe, the aquifers, the growing desertization of the planet, the injustice, the hatred, the irrationality,and the racism, requires adding emotional education into the school curricula.

Technical competence is indispensable to enable Third World people to enter the age of high technology. Excellence in education is a necessity for the rest of the world. Education must assume responsibility for enculturation. A crisis in values is a crisis in culture. This original formulation, of both education, and of culture, would be useful for the training of teachers. There are, today, quick and very effective techniques for the removal of emotional blocks that interfere with self actualization. Intelligence should no longer be, as the Venezuelan educator, Luis Alberto Machado, argues, "a human right most violated in the world we live in."

The most advanced knowledge, in all the fields of learning, can be abridged in lessons (modules) to be offered by means of reciprocal co-tutoring. Consultants of excellence in mastery of humanistic education, would organize the educational contents offered in schools today, in modules, prepared for reciprocal co-tutoring, at all the educational levels, Humanistic education requires the complement of co facilitation to remove from the mind of the student, emotional blocks created by experiences of pain, of extreme deprivation, of all kinds of traumaticities.

Reciprocal co-facilitation is a low cost procedure that provides an opportunity, that now only the wealthy can afford and enjoy, at very high cost, in the offices of professional psychotherapists. Under the auspices of the Fulbright Program, we had the opportunity to work at the Universidad del Norte in Barranquilla, Colombia. It was in the design of a school without walls, in one of the poorest places on the planet. Its name, Zona Negra, is taken from the fact that sewage, (aguas negras) runs through the streets of that community, and in some places, forms pools in which the children often swim and play.

This proposal would transform education into reciprocal co-tutoring and cofacilitation. The cofacilitation modules have been included in the manual, "Comunicacion es Felicidad," an effective low cost instrument for emotional and cognitive education.. This is proposed as a solution to the waste of human potentialities in underdeveloped countries, as well as for deprived sectors of developed ones.

Doctor Agustin Lombana, Executive Director of the Educational Commission of Exchange between Colombia and United States, comments on the design in the following words., "When I finished reading this Manual, I realized that it is very relevant to the circumstances in Colombia, my home land. But then, as days went by, I realized that this Manual is not only for the present time, nor only for Colombia, it has relevance for all humanity. Human values are universal. Our Colombian society needs these values more today than in its entire history. For this reason, this Manual is very useful for all of us."

BIBLIOGRAPHY

Abelardo, Diaz Alfaro, Terrazo, San Juan, Biblioteca de Autores Puertoriquenos, 1947.

Adler, Alfred, Individual Psychology, N. Y. Harper, 1956

Alegria, Ciro El Mundo es Ancho y Ajeno (The World is Broad and Alien"

Amato, Pedro Munoz, Informe al Gobernador, Sobre Los Dereches Civiles
en Puerto Rico. 1958

Ashley, M. F.-Montagu, Man's Most Dangerous Myth The Fallacy of Race,
New York: World Publishing Co., 1964

Benedict, Ruth. Patterns of Culture, New York. Mentor 1943

Berne, Erik, Games People Play, New York Grove, 1966

Bettelheim, B. Love is not Enough, New York: Avon, 1960

Bruner, J. S. etal. A Study of Thinking. New York: Wiley, 1958

142

Castro Caycedo, German, El Hueco, Bogota, Planeta, 1989

Chomsky, Noam, Syntactic Structures, Mouton, 1957

Davis, Kingsley, Extreme Social Isolation of a Child American Journal
of Sociology XLV (January, 1940.)

de Mello, Anthony, La Illuminacion, Buenos Aires, Ediciones Karma, 1992

De Waal, Frans B. M., Scientific American, Edition February 2000

Direnzo, Gordon J. ed. Concepts, Theory and Explanation, New York,
Random House, 1966

Einstein, Albert, "Why Socialism": New York Monthly Review, 1949

Frankl, E. El Hombre en Busca del Sentido, Barcelona, Editorial
Herder, 1994

Freeman, Derek Margaret Mead and Somoa (The Making and Unmaking of
an Anthropological Myth) Harvard Press, 1983

Freire, Paolo. Education for Critical Consciousness. New York: Seabury, 1973

Pedagogia del Oprimido, Montevideo. Tierras Nuevan, 1968

Freud, Ana The Ego and the Mechanisms of Defense. New York
:
Freud, Sigmund, ed. Strachey. London: Hogarth Press, 1913-1916
Standard Edition of theComplete Psychological Works of Sigmund Freud   The Question of Lay Analysis. New York, 1953
Psycho Pathology of Every Day Life in the Basic Writings of Sigmund   Freud, NewYork Modern Library, 1938

Galeano, Eduardo, Por las Venas Abiertas del Continente

German, Castro Caycedo

Gunder-Frank, Andre, Lumpen-Burguesia y lumpen-Desarrollo, Mexico, Era
1971. Reorient It: Global Economy in the Asian Age University of
California Press,

Hammonds, Peter Physical Anthropology and Archaeology New York,
MacMillan, 1965.

Hansen, Earl Parker Puerto Rico, Country of Wonders

Harris, M. Patterns of Race in the Americas, New York, Columbia
University Press, 1976

Hartman, H., Ego Psychology and the Problem of Adaptation, New York,
International University Press, 1958

Herdandez, Carmen Dolores "Illustrious Illiterate" El Nuevo Dia, July
27,2000, pg 141

Horowitz, L. "Historia de la Sociologia del Conocimiento EUDEBA, 1964,pg. 11.

Ianni, Octavio

Iglesias, Cesar Andreu, "La Segunda Generacion", en Cosas de Aqui, El
Imparcial, 1964

Itard, J. M. G. The Wild Boy of Averyron New York, Appleton Century,1962

Jones, Ernest. The Life and Work of Sigmund Freud, New York, Basic
Book, 1957, pg 292.

Jung, Carl Gustav. "Simbologia del Espiritu", Mexico Fondo de Cultura,1951

Keller, Helen, Story of my Life, New York, Doubleday, 1954

Kelly, George Psychology of Personal Constructs vol. 2, New York,Norton, 1955

Khun, Thomas The Rise of Scientific Revolutions. Chicago, University of
Chicago Press, 1970

Klein, Melanie Mourning: Its Relation to Manic Depressive States in
Contribution to Psychoanalysis. New York, McGraw Hill, 1948

Kluhkhon, Clyde, Personality andNature, Society and Culture, 1957

Lagner, Susan, Philosophy in a New Key New York Mentor, 1956

Lambert, Wallace Language, Psychology, and Culture: (Language science and   national development) 01 April, 1972

Lai,Singh Joseph Amrito and Zingg, Robert, Wolf Children and Feral Man
Anchor Books, Hamden, CT., 1966

Linton, Ralph, The Study of Man: An Introduction, New York, Appleton Century,   1936, pg. 35

Lombana, Agustin Prologue of "Comunicacion es Felicidad". 1991

Luria, A. R. Lenguaje y Pensamiento, Barcelona, Conducta Humana, 1980

Machado, Luis Alberto "El Derecho de Ser Inteligente", Caracas, Seix Barral,1979

Marcuse, Herbert Eros and Civilization, New York, Vintage, 1961

Maquiavelo, Nicolas, El Principe

Marquez, Garcia, Cien Anos de Soledad, Bogota, Oveja Negra, 1963
"Cronica de un Concierto Roquero", Universidad de Puerto Rico Dialogo,
Oct. 1997, pg. 14

Marx, Karl "Economic and Philosophical Manuscripts" (Moscow, Foreign
Language,1959

Mead, Margaret Love Under the Palm Trees

Merton, R. K. Social Theory and ocial Structure Glencoe, The Free Press
1956, On the Shoulders of Giants

Molano, Alfredo Aguas Arriba: Entre la Coca y el Oro, 1998

Morris, Charles W. Sign, Language and Behavior, New York, Prentice Hall,1946

Mower, H. Behavior and the Symbolic Process New York, Wiley, 1965

Murphy, M. G. The Development of Peirce Philosophy, 1961

O'Neill, Ana Maria. Etica Para la Era Atomica, Rio Piedras, U.P.R.,1976

Ortega, Gasset J. La Rebelion de las Masas, Madrid, Revista de Occidente,1936

Packard, Vance The Hidden Persuaders New York: McKay, 1957

Parsons, Talcott Structure of Social Action New York, 1937

Peck, M. Scott, M.D., The Road Less Traveled, Simon & Shuster, nd.

Prenant, Marcel Razay Racismo Mexico, Fondo de Cultura, 1939

Purke, William W. Self Concept and School Achievement New Jersey,
Englewood Cliff, 1970

Reyes, Gerardo Biography of Don Julio Mario ediciones B, 2004

Rodo, Jose Enrique Ariel, Motevideo, 1944

Rosen, John N. Direct Psycho-Analysis, New York, Grune & Stratton,1953

Sapir, Edward Culture Genuine and Spurious

Saxe, John The Blind Men and the Elephant version of Famous Indian Legend.
McGraw-Hill, 1963

Sartre, Jean Paul Existential Psycho-analysis, New York, Gateway, 1966

Seda Bonilla, Eduardo Requiem para una Cultura. Rio Piedras, Bayoan,1972
Social Change and Personality Evanston, North Western University Press,
1973
Los Derechos Civiles en la Cultura Puertorriquena Rio Piedras:Editorial
Universitaria, 1963. edicion revisada: Rio Piedras Ediciones Bayoan,1973

"The Paradox of the Unmeltable Pseudo-Vicissitudes of Being 'Puerto Rican"
in Melus, V1, #13, Fall, 1979
"Ser en el Quehacer vs Ser en el Tener" Revista Plerus, 1984
"Asimilacion Co-Cultural: Urgencia Para Las Minorias Estigmatizadas"
Mexico, America Indigena, 1986
Tres Formas de Aprender a Ser", Revista Homines, Vol.11, 1 Marzo,1987
"La Cuestion de la Ensenanza del Ingles en las Escuelas Publicas de
Puerto Rico" Cuadernos del Idioma, U.P.R. Marzo, 1988
"El Efecto Rashomon", Cuadernos de Idioma, U.P.R., 1989
Lumpenizacion, Rio Piedras, Bayoan, 1989
Educacion Valores, Salud Mental Rio Piedras, Bayoan, 1989
Comunicacion Es Felicidad, Rio Piedras, Bayoan, 1991
"Libertinaje Epistemico", U.P.R. Revista de Ciencias Sociales,Vol,XXX, 1
2, 1993
De la Familia Nuclear al Aparejamiento", Revista Grito Cultural,Num.4,1994
"La Ley 54", Revista America, Ano 9, num 10, 1997
"Quien Mato a tu Hijo?" Grito Cultural, Num.3, 1999
Pseudo Ethniticity is a Collective Hallucination' Carribean Studies, University
of Puerto Rico

Silberman, Charles E. Crisis in the Classroom NewYork, Random House, 1970

Singh, Joseph Amrito Lai and Zingg, Robert, Wolf Children and Feral Man,Anchor
Books, Hamden, CT., 1966

Skinner, Burrhus Frederic. Beyond Freedom and Dignity 1971

Smith, Adam The Wealth of Nations Prometheus Books, 1991

Sorman, Guey "Los Verdaderos Pensadores de Nuestrra Tiempo" (The True
Thinkers of Our Time) Colombia, Seix Barral, 1995

Sorokin, Pitirim A. Sociedad, Cultura y Personalidad Madrid, Aguilar,1960

Sorman, Guey "Los Verdaderos Pensadores de Nuestrra Tiempo" Colombia,
Seix Barral, 1995

Spitz, R. A. Hospitalism, an inquiry into the Genesis of Psychiatric Conditions in
Early Childhood, The Psychoanalytic Study of the Child. New York,
International University Press, 1945

Stuckert, Robert article: "Race Mixtures; The African Ancestry of White Americans"
Paul Hammond ed.."Physical Anthropology and Archae-ology" New York

MacMillan, 1965

Sullivan, Harry S. Conceptions of Modern Psychiatry, Mouton, 1953

Szasz, Thomas, The Myth of Mental Illness

Thompson, Clara, Psychoanalysis Evolution and Development, NewYork, 1950

Toch, H. and Smith, H.C., Social Perception. Van Nostrand, 1968

Unamuno, de Miguel. Letters: Madrid, 1972

UNESCO: "Declaracion Sobre Raza y Racismo" 1952, The Declaration on Race of the American Society" Sept. issue, pg..27, 1995

Vernon, M.D. The Psychology of Perception, Penguin, 1962

Weber, Marx Protestant Ethics and the Spirit of Capitalism New York, Scribner
and Sons, 1958

Wilber, Ken The Quest for New Paradygm. Boston, Shambala, 1990,pg.55
"How to Save the Earth", Time Magazine, Sring, 2000

Wise, Brian Muchas Vidas Muchos Maestros, Madrid, Bolsillo, 1995
"Lazos de Amor", Biblioteca de Bolsillo, 1997

Zenon, Hector Bermudez article in "Revista Grito Cultural", #1, 1998

ISBN 1-41205126-6

Made in the USA
Middletown, DE
16 February 2015